DISCOVERING HIDDEN PROFIT

DISCOVERING HIDDEN PROFIT

Extended Value Stream Decision Making

PETER J. MARKS | ROBERT O. MARTICHENKO

Printed in the United States of America
Signature Book Printing, www.sbpbooks.com

ISBN-978-0-9970308-3-9

Book Design by AuthorSupport.com
Copy Editing by Carole Boyd
Illustrations by Weston DeWolff

DEDICATION

This book is dedicated to all the people with whom we have worked,
from whom we have learned, and with whom we have engaged
in lively discussions about organizational development.

They all made valuable contributions to this book,
and for that we are eternally grateful.

Peter and Robert

TABLE OF CONTENTS

Profit for the Taking

"…this is not a competition between departments."

—SUE ARMSTRONG

There is an ancient eastern proverb that states *Where profit is, loss is hidden nearby.* The corollary is also true in that *Where loss is, profit is hidden nearby.*

Discovering Hidden Profit leverages both of these powerful statements by providing a methodology to connect people to business processes in order to eliminate loss and discover new profit opportunities.

This can be accomplished without changing your current business strategy, introducing new products, adding to sales and marketing budgets, or having to increase operating cost in your supply chain.

The path to discovering and extracting hidden profit rests within viewing the organization from a new perspective, one where we go from being focused on single-process optimization to viewing the business as a *total system* formed when we connect people and processes.

This is the essence of *Discovering Hidden Profit*, where you identify and capture incremental profit opportunity by simply viewing and acting upon your business from a total-system perspective.

No matter what business you are in today, you are experiencing disruptions. Business landscapes are changing fundamentally, and our job as leaders is now to anticipate, keep up with, and attempt to stay ahead of these disruptions. Ironically though, with all of this disruption, the game of business itself has not changed. We must continue to *maximize customer value at the lowest possible total cost,* all while showing respect for people and our communities.

So what is different? New and agile competitors, globalization of our supply chains, and e-commerce are easy examples. Changing customer expectations and behavior characterized by endless choices, customization, rapid delivery require-ments, and omni-channel shopping experiences are others. And the list goes on . . .

What is the result of all this disruption? At a high level, these disruptions and the resulting complexity have evolved faster than the development of our organiza-tions' business processes and management systems, which has negatively affected most businesses. This is why it's time for a fundamental shift in our thinking and actions as leaders.

Business leaders have always recognized the potential for better operational and financial performance if leaders across core processes and functional areas worked together more cohesively. To do this, leaders and managers in an organization need to see and think about the business from a *holistic business-wide* point of view. We need to be *system-wide thinkers*. We need to understand that an organization is similar to an organism — action, reaction, and results are difficult to predict. In contrast, we also need to embrace that organizational functions are similar to a *machine* — a series of connected processes that form a whole, a system of gears that act as a whole to produce some planned and expected outcome. To that end, we need to implement operating principles that emphasize *customer value* and *total costs* at a business system-wide level. We need to focus on profit as a function of revenue and total cost from a holistic point of view across the entire business enterprise. We need to make profit predictable.

We need to discover and extract hidden profit that currently exists within our operations but is hidden because of the fact that we are not business-wide systems thinkers.

This book focuses on how to accomplish these objectives and dramatically improve company performance through what we call "*Supply-Chain Advancement.*"

Supply-Chain Advancement (SCA) is a business-improvement methodology that discovers and extracts hidden profit by connecting core processes to achieve Advanced Supply-Chain Performance.

Now, at this point you are probably saying, "Oh, this is a book on supply-chain management. I should probably hand this off to my supply-chain executive!" Nothing could be farther from the truth. This book is for you, a CEO or executive leader, as we are talking about comprehensive business improvement across the entire organization. This is about significant and measured business results achieved both operationally and financially, where these potential results currently exist within your core processes.

Let's expand on our definition of SCA.

Supply-Chain Advancement (SCA) is a business-improvement methodology that discovers and extracts hidden profit by connecting and integrating the core business processes of Business Strategy, Product Life-Cycle Management, Sales and Marketing, and Supply-Chain Operations in order to achieve Advanced Supply-Chain Performance.

With this expanded definition in mind, what is Advanced Supply-Chain Performance?

Advanced Supply-Chain Performance is the overall performance (and profit) that an organization is giving up when core business processes are not connected, when managers are focused on single processes only and are not working towards the common goal of maximizing customer value at the lowest possible total cost to the business system wide.

Advanced Supply-Chain Performance is the current supply-chain performance of the organization + the opportunity that exists today if we connect core processes of the business.

More specifically, Advanced Supply-Chain Performance is the business performance we will achieve if we focus our attention on having the *right strategy* to deliver and sell only the *right products* while being supported with the *right supply-chain operations* across the business system wide. Building upon this, imagine a business where all of your products exceed customer expectations, where all of your products flow continuously from source to customer, and where all of your products produce a visible and competitive level of profit for the organization.

SCA and the action plans in this book will roll out the methodology to help accomplish this goal.

To get started, and to make sure we are experiencing the same business environment, here's a short, high-level diagnostic.

Do any of these leadership experiences or situations hit close to home?

SCA - CEO DIAGNOSTIC

☐ You have invested in Lean, Six Sigma, or similar philosophies but have not sustained significant, measurable results across the entire organization.

☐ Leaders across the organization do not collaborate effectively, resulting in function-based decisions that generate organizational waste.

☐ Business models, technology, product introductions, customer expectations, and distribution channels have changed faster than you expected, and your core operations were not prepared for it.

☐ Your leadership team does not have a deep understanding of the entire business-wide system, resulting in decisions that diminish customer value and add waste to the business.

☐ Your business processes lack business-wide performance measures, and your employee performance systems (KPIs) drive functional behaviors and decisions that are suboptimal to the overall business.

☐ You have a complex array of products, but you are convinced that not all products produce a reasonable contribution to profit.

☐ You often feel the solutions to your big problems rest in restructuring the organization, buying new technologies, or outsourcing functions.

☐ You often believe the instability in your supply chain is caused by erratic customer demand and/or your inability to forecast accurately.

☐ Your cash is tied up in inventory that moves painfully slowly through the supply chain.

☐ You don't know exactly what to do going forward, but your gut tells you there simply needs to be a better way.

If you can relate to any of these statements, we ask you read on. This book offers the framework and methodology to inspire and guide you to further business improvement that will tackle these challenges.

As authors, we make several promises to you. First, we will not inundate you with concepts and theories that are not practical to implement. Second, we will focus on building upon your current strategies, building upon any work you have completed to develop a culture of continuous improvement. Last, we promise that real, measurable, and significant business results will derive from this work. It will not always be easy, but focusing on Supply-Chain Advancement will take you to the next level of business performance required in today's world of constant disruption.

With these promises, we ask something from you. First, understand that this is not a book about supply-chain management. This is a book about business management, focusing on overall business performance. The ideas in this book need to be understood by <u>all</u> executives inside your organization in addition to your supply-chain leaders in order to begin the journey of cross-functional, business-wide system thinking. Second, try not to reject these concepts as being "too hard" to implement. The fact is, this is the work that may very well determine which organizations survive and thrive in the coming decades.

With those expectations set and promises made, let's get started.

ACT 1

Foundational Thinking

Many leaders wear masks that define them as their functional personalities and the roles their functions play in the overall staged production of the business. Consequently, the CEO has a cast of leaders that are focused on their own part of the production but not on the outcome of the production as a whole.

The Business Problem

*"...we have to have business models
that allow us to operate quickly."*

—MICHAEL EDMUNDS

If there is one thing we have learned as business leaders, it's that people do not spend enough time trying to understand the problems they are trying to solve. This lack of problem-solving discipline leads to frequent changes in strategy and leadership meddling in the day-to-day business, resulting in confusion and frustration at all levels of the organization. Therefore, it is important that we first understand the problem we are trying to solve through Supply-Chain Advancement (SCA).

A premise of Supply-Chain Advancement is that enterprise-wide business improvements will not be realized until leaders and managers collaborate across the entire business in order to connect core processes, drive customer value holistically, and eliminate waste systematically.

But why is this so important, and why is it important now? To answer these questions, we need to explore today's business problems.

THE CUSTOMER AND THE EXTERNAL ENVIRONMENT

In business, no matter what problem we are trying to solve, we should always start with our customer. Listening to the voice of our customer is key to finding optimum business solutions. By doing so, we will solve problems in ways that generate the *maximum customer value at the lowest possible total cost to our organization.*

Customers now want *more value for less.* This may seem unrealistic to sustain in the long term, but it is a harsh reality in all industries. Here's a short list of today's customer expectations:

* Constantly higher value and lower prices
* Superior and increased quality
* Faster innovation cycle for product features and performance
* Increased personalization and product customization
* Extended service offerings and lifetime product support
* Reduced delivery times and no-hassle return policies

There was a time when providing such additional value could command a premium. Those days are over. The above list of customer demands is simply the price of admission in many markets. How have businesses responded to these ever increasing customer expectations?

If we consolidate our reactions and solutions to these increasing customer expectations, it comes down to two words: *increased complexity.* We have made our businesses more and more complex in order to meet customer expectations while attempting to remain profitable. This complexity has created a long list of unintended consequences and unplanned waste in the business system wide.

Let's look at a few of the customer demands and our responses that have created turmoil inside our organizations and demonstrate how our development of people and processes has failed to keep up:

■ **Lower Prices**: The market determines the price, so profit is now a function of our ability to design, source, make, and distribute products at the target cost respective to the market price. In order to achieve this, we have globalized our supply chains in pursuit of cheaper inputs and lower production costs. This globalization has resulted in increased lead times and greater overall management oversight. Our people and processes were not ready for this additional supply-chain complexity, and the result has been increased inventories, reduced customer-fill rates, and, potentially, higher overall operating cost. We say potentially because we are less aware of our costs today as the increased complexity has reduced our ability to understand total costs.

■ **Endless Variation**: Customers expect more—more features, more options, more benefits—but they don't expect to pay more. In response our product-development functions create more products with more features and more options. This has resulted in product proliferation that exceeds the ability of our people and processes to manage it. As a result our supply chains and order-fulfillment processes have become more complex in the form of increased inventory and greater variation in production processes. We may believe we have done the right thing and that we are still making money with all of these new products. However, once again, we aren't entirely sure because the additional complexity has exceeded our ability to capture profit contribution by product.

> **We have made our businesses more and more complex in order to meet customer expectations while attempting to remain profitable.**

In addition, because our product-development cycles are moving so fast we are unable to collaborate well across core functions of the business. This results in new-product launches that fail to hit sales targets, field failures, and overall confusion and frustration within the organization. In short, we have tried to provide additional variety and services to our customers without sufficiently developing the necessary core competencies for doing it well, resulting in wasted resources, excessive costs, and poor financial performance.

■ **Reduced Lead Times and Enhanced Flexibility**: Today's customers expect ever faster delivery and response times. What's perplexing is that our efforts to chase lower supply and production costs have accomplished the exact opposite. Global supply chains have extended lead times, increased process and management complexity, increased process variation, reduced supply-chain responsiveness, increased inventories, and expanded overall operating costs. Many organizations have implemented lean manufacturing techniques in an attempt to reduce lead times, but most of these lean initiatives are not connected to the outbound supply-chain and order-fulfillment processes, so any gains the customer would care about have not been realized. In other words, we have built new on-ramps to a freeway that is gridlocked. It's no wonder that such efforts haven't produced the significant enterprise-wide business results that lean thinking is capable of achieving.

Figure 1 — *The External Environment and the Internal Reaction*

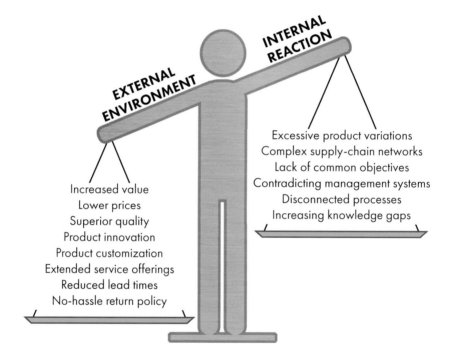

Our process and management systems have not kept up
with the challenges of the external environment.

In summary, our attempts to meet changing customer demands have created increased complexity (much of it unplanned and wasteful) by introducing excessive product variation, long lead times between suppliers and manufacturing locations, and new service offerings without sufficient fulfillment competencies. Our management systems have not kept up with this additional complexity; our people's knowledge has not kept up. This has resulted in an abundance of operational waste and missed opportunities relative to meeting customers' needs. Simply put, we are missing revenue opportunities while adding costs to the business. This is a problem, as an equation of reduced revenues with rising costs is not sustainable.

Now, are we saying that we should dismantle the global supply chain? Are we saying customers should temper their expectations? Are we saying that we should stop creating innovative and creative products?

Absolutely not.

As authors and business leaders, we are saying that this new world requires a different type of thinking. This new business environment requires business decision makers to understand the intended and unintended consequences of business decisions and the resulting planned and unplanned complexity. Proactively we need to understand and reduce the risk of unintended consequences and unplanned complexity of our decisions. We need very specific goals, operating principles, and a management system that will support this new world of supply-chain complexity. Core business processes need to collaborate, managers need to think from a business-wide system point of view, and everyone needs to understand that all decisions will manifest themselves as either customer value or waste.

REALITY CHECK

Before we move to the next chapters and begin outlining Supply-Chain Advancement, you need to know that we understand the challenges that senior business leaders face today. We do not underestimate these challenges. Running our own businesses and spending time with other executives from a variety of industries, we find many of the same concerns. We know that as a business leader:

- ☐ You have great products and services and effective strategies, but revenue growth and margins are below your expectations.
- ☐ You want to build on current strategies but do not want to change directions or restructure your organization again.
- ☐ You are not afraid of complexity, but your business is becoming more complex faster than your management system is able to accommodate it.
- ☐ You don't like unpredictability, but you are continuously being surprised, which disrupts your ability to focus on the long term.

☐ You want your business managers to focus on innovation and high performance, but they seem to focus more on cost reduction within a single process and preventing service failures from happening.

☐ You want to see clear, measurable, business-wide results from your strategic initiatives and operational improvement efforts, but you struggle to see visible bottom-line results from your investments.

It's time to address these challenges. As business leaders we need to move toward our long-term visions while still producing short-term results. We need our organizational structures and management systems to drive collaboration and cross-functional decision making. We need process improvements to become institutionalized into our management systems, and we need a simple way to benchmark, measure, and assess performance.

> **We need our organizational structures and management systems to drive collaboration and cross-functional decision making. We need process improvements to become institutionalized into our management systems, and we need a simple way to benchmark, measure, and assess performance.**

In an attempt to achieve these goals many companies have been reorganized and restructured, usually more than once. In the end, however, the anticipated collaboration, enhanced efficiencies, and market responsiveness do not materialize. Organizational structure isn't the issue. It's not about who reports to whom.

To improve collaboration and drive business-wide systems thinking, you don't need to restructure your organization. You need a simple roadmap that everyone in the organization can align around to move forward. This is what SCA provides.

Will Supply-Chain Advancement be easy to accomplish? Perhaps not, as it requires people to look at the business from a new perspective, and it requires leaders and managers to work collaboratively towards a common set of objectives. This means we need to view the organization holistically and connect and relate the core business processes of Business Strategy, Product Life-Cycle Management, Sales and Marketing, and Supply-Chain Operations.

This connection of these four core business processes is the most significant business opportunity organizations need to pursue. It is the last frontier for meaningful business improvement and the management of all the disruption around us.

Whether your organization is fighting for survival or is healthy and looking for innovative ways to produce additional value, Supply-Chain Advancement is the methodology that provides the path forward.

SCA Axioms and Assumptions

CHAPTER | 2

"…the greatest contributing factor to the success of our supply chain transformation was an end-to-end commitment from senior management on down."

—CHARLIE ARMSTRONG

A s mentioned earlier, it requires great discipline to devote the correct amount of time to understanding the problem we are trying to solve. This allows us to answer the all-important question of *why* we should do this work. To answer the *why* question fully, we need to identify the external and internal pressures we face, and we need to know the assumptions and foundational thinking that brings us to our recommended solution. More specifically, Supply-Chain Advancement (SCA) certainly provides the *what* to do, but in the spirit of disciplined problem solving, we should first answer the *why*. That is, *why* is Supply-Chain Advancement the methodology we should embrace today in order to meet our current challenges head on?

To answer this question, we need to understand several axioms and assumptions up front so that all SCA recommendations will have a foundational platform from which they originate.

Before we get started with our SCA axioms, we would like to introduce a few terms that we will use consistently throughout the book.

SCA COMMONLY USED TERMS

* **Business Strategy:** Business Strategy is the core process that develops and sets the course for the business derived from the mission, vision, values, and extensive market and customer research.

* **Product Life-Cycle Management:** Product and service life-cycle planning and management includes the inception of a product or service, product design and engineering, planning for material sourcing, planning for manufacturing, planning for distribution, value-added services, and ultimate product retirement or disposal.

* **Sales and Marketing:** Sales and Marketing entails planning of potential and targeted customer segments, development of distribution and sales channels, planning for multiple customer-delivery techniques (omni-channel), sales promotions, pricing strategies, and product-demand and forecast planning.

* **Supply-Chain Operations:** Supply-Chain Operations (Supply Chain) are the operational elements of order fulfillment, namely the physical flow of material and supporting information. This includes material sourcing, inbound logistics, manufacturing, finished-goods distribution, and all information-flow processes relating to planning and executing these supply-chain and logistics processes.

* **Extended Value Stream:** This is the total system created when we connect business strategy, product life-cycle management, sales and marketing, and supply-chain operations in order to maximize customer value at the lowest possible total cost.

* **End-to-End Supply Chain:** This is the total system created when we connect all supply-chain and logistics processes, starting at the customer and working upstream through manufacturing and into our supplier base.

With these common terms established, let's move into SCA axioms.

SCA AXIOM 1: ALL BUSINESS DECISIONS ARE ULTIMATELY MANIFESTED IN THE SUPPLY CHAIN.

Business decisions will be made in every part of a business; however, the resulting value and waste created by these decisions are manifested in the supply chain. In addition, these business decisions have intended and unintended consequences. Such decisions produce planned (required) and unplanned (not required) complexity in the supply chain. Therefore, an abundance of critical information needed to improve business performance, increase customer value, and eliminate waste rests inside the supply chain. This means our overall supply-chain performance has a strong correlation with overall business performance and provides a feedback mechanism for all business decisions made in all parts of the business. Consequently, the supply chain is a largely untapped reservoir of information and intelligence offering the root causes and possible solutions to many of our biggest business problems.

***Figure 2** — Supply-Chain Performance Provides Critical Feedback*

All business decisions are ultimately manifested in the supply chain.

In short, all good deeds and all sins end up in the supply chain.

SCA provides the methodology to leverage supply-chain performance in order to prioritize business-improvement activities.

SCA AXIOM 2: EXTENDED VALUE-STREAM THINKING DISCOVERS HIDDEN PROFIT.

We create an *Extended Value Stream* when we connect the core processes of Business Strategy, Product Life-Cycle Management, Sales and Marketing, and Supply-Chain Operations. This extended value stream is a total system that ultimately produces value for the customer or waste in the system based on the effectiveness and rigor of the connection points. Managing the extended value stream needs to be accomplished holistically, recognizing that an action in one core process will have a direct and immediate impact on another core process.

Once extended value-stream thinking is embraced, managers and leaders will have extensive and deep market, customer, and cross-functional knowledge and experience to make effective decisions. They will then maximize customer value at the lowest possible total cost to the business, where *total cost* is defined as the system-wide, long-term total cost of a decision.

SCA provides the methodology to create the Extended Value Stream.

Note: For purposes of SCA we refer to core business processes as business strategy, product life-cycle management, sales and marketing, and supply-chain

Figure 3 — *Extended Value Stream*

The Extended Value Stream is the sum of Business Strategy, Product Life-Cycle Management, Sales & Marketing, and Supply-Chain Operations.

operations. In subsequent chapters we will delve deeply into these core business processes and their impact on Advanced Supply-Chain Performance. When we talk about the "Extended Value Stream" we are referring to the connecting and relating of these four core business processes to make holistic systems-wide decisions that are optimal for the business as a whole. We fully recognize there are other extremely important processes within an organization: HR, IT, Legal, Admin, etc. The recommendations going forward relative to SCA can all be applied within any function of the organization.

SCA AXIOM 3: SUPPLY CHAIN-CENTRIC DECISION MAKING WILL DRIVE EXTENDED VALUE-STREAM THINKING AND REDUCE COMPLEXITY.

Extended Value-Stream thinking is not about the charisma or talents of particular leaders, but rather it is about having a management system that drives and sustains supply chain-centric thinking and advanced supply-chain decision making.

Traditional supply-chain decision making is focused on single-process optimization and will result in both intended and unintended consequences across the extended value stream. These consequences will drive required and non-required complexity into the end-to-end supply chain, where the non-required complexities are pure waste.

Advanced Supply Chain-Centric Decision Making proactively eliminates unintended consequences, thereby eliminating non-required complexities and resulting waste. It is about asking, *How will this decision add value to the customer or create unplanned complexity and unintended waste in the supply chain?* Asking this question on a habitual basis introduces a supply chain-centric view of the organization,

> **Advanced Supply Chain-Centric Decision Making proactively eliminates unintended consequences, thereby eliminating non-required complexities and resulting waste.**

which is the first step toward solving many of the big problems we face today. We will thus proactively work to avoid introducing new complexity and waste into the supply chain. Supply Chain-Centric Decision Making will break down functional barriers, foster collaboration, improve supply-chain performance, and ultimately improve overall business performance by creating an organization that maximizes value at the lowest possible total cost across the extended value stream.

SCA provides the methodology to create a management system that fosters Supply Chain-Centric Decision Making.

Figure 4 — *Traditional vs. Advanced Supply-Chain Decision Making*

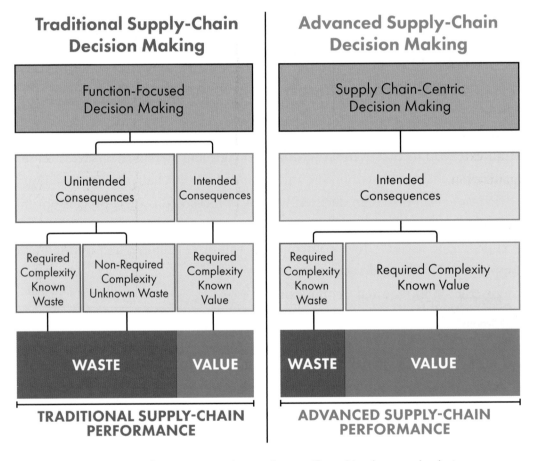

All business decisions are ultimately manifested in the supply chain.

SCA AXIOM 4: SUPPLY-CHAIN ADVANCEMENT ENABLES ADVANCED SUPPLY-CHAIN PERFORMANCE.

Advanced Supply-Chain Performance (ASCP) is the increased operational and financial performance that an organization realizes by implementing

SCA and integrating and connecting the core business processes of Business Strategy, Product Life-Cycle Management, Sales and Marketing, and Supply-Chain Operations.

Further, Advanced Supply-Chain Performance is the business result achieved when an organization implements SCA to capitalize on supply-chain profit potential that currently exists but is not being captured. ASCP is measured operationally by improving the Ten Rights holistically across the extended value stream in order to deliver 1) the right products, 2) to the right customers, 3) in the right quantities, 4) in the right quality, 5) at the right times, 6) from the right sources, 7) at the right prices, 8) at the right total cost, 9) with the right services, 10) all within the right amount of required complexity (effort).

ASCP is measured financially through improvement in 1) new revenues, 2) reduced operating costs, 3) improved working-capital position, and 4) reduced overall extended value-stream lead times, all resulting in increased profit to the organization.

Figure 5 — Advanced Supply-Chain Performance

Advanced Supply-Chain Performance will be achieved
by connecting the core business processes.

In summary, *Advanced Supply-Chain Performance is the measured incremental business performance we realize when we integrate core business processes holistically to achieve the Ten Rights across the extended value stream of the organization in order to maximize customer value at the lowest possible total cost to the organization.*

SCA will detail the step-by-step activities that create a system to be implemented to achieve Advanced Supply-Chain Performance.

We will go into more detail relative to ASCP and the Ten Rights in Chapter 4.

SCA AXIOM 5: TIME IS MONEY.

As the old saying goes, time is money. Relative to business this is true because time is only made up of two variables: Value and Waste. In other words, either we are adding value to our products and moving our products closer to our customer, or we are not. Any time our processes or products are not having value added to them (or not moving to the customer) is considered waste. Therefore, it is logical to measure the effectiveness of a business by how long it takes us to do things. With this in mind, from an SCA point of view, the overall performance of an organization can be measured by the total lead time of the extended value stream.

Figure 6 — *Extended Value-Stream Lead Time*

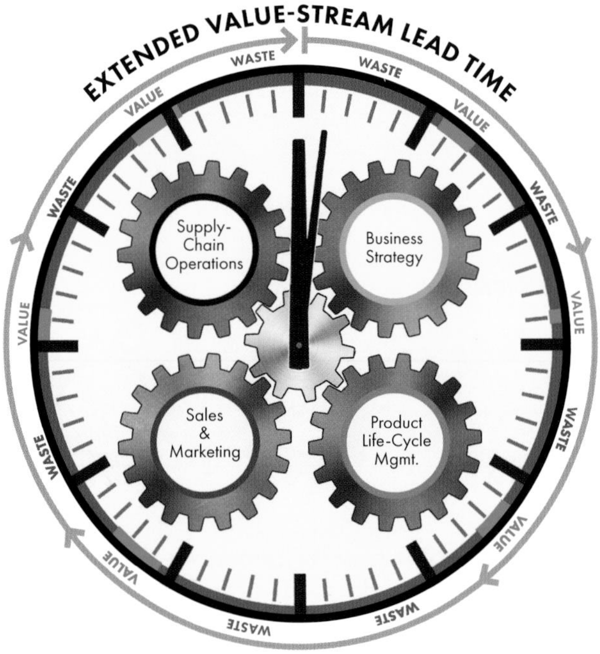

Lead Time is only made up of two variables: value and waste.

SCA provides the methodology to visualize, understand, and reduce total extended value-stream lead time.

Now that we have outlined the foundational elements of SCA, let's move to looking at SCA and SCA implementation at a strategic level.

SCA – The Engine Inside the System

CHAPTER | 3

"…companies have to become more nimble and create customization capabilities that differentiate your products. This makes complexity a growth enabler, not just something to complain about."

—RICK SATHER

The first two chapters summarized the foundational platform of Supply-Chain Advancement (SCA). We will now use this chapter to outline SCA focus areas, enablers, and the implementation steps for successful realization of hidden profit, addressing them at a strategic level. We will then use the rest of the book to delve into the tactical details of each recommended action.

As described in the introduction, *SCA is a business-improvement methodology that discovers and extracts hidden profit by connecting core processes to achieve advanced supply-chain performance.*

The question we now need to ask is how does SCA accomplish this?

SCA accomplishes its goals of uncovering currently existing hidden profit by implementing supply chain-centric operating principles to connect core business processes, establishing a disciplined management-system structure, leveraging supply-chain performance as a problem-solving feedback loop, and achieving supply chain-centric decision making in order to realize measured business improvements across the extended value stream.

At this point we will discuss each of these concepts at a strategic level and then go into the details in upcoming chapters.

SCA FOCUS AREAS AND ENABLERS

Supply-Chain Advancement is based on the SCA axiom that a business is a system where all gears (processes, functions) in the system are interdependent and together holistically play a role in the overall outcomes and results of business decisions. Consequently, enablers for SCA also need to form a system, or machine, that will become part of the overall management system of the organization.

> **Supply-Chain Advancement is based on the SCA axiom that a business is a system where all gears (processes, functions) in the system are interdependent and together holistically play a role in the overall outcomes and results of business decisions.**

SCA has three main focus areas of work that cascade into *activities* to complete the SCA methodology. For the purpose of describing these focus areas, we will refer to them as *gears*. The term gear is chosen to indicate that these are parts of a system that are interdependent and create a whole when connected. As well, this means that we will be doing work in all three gears concurrently. This is important to note so we don't fall into the trap of feeling as if all actions are consecutive in nature. For example, we can easily start training people in SCA at the same time as we roll out SCA operating principles within core processes.

THE THREE MAIN FOCUS AREAS (GEARS) OF SCA ARE:

1 **SCA Gear 1: Establish Transparency and Demonstrate Full Intent:**
Goal Setting + Management-System Alignment

2 **SCA Gear 2: Remove the Mask and Unite the Cast:**
Core-Process Connection + SCA Operating-Principle Implementation

3 **SCA Gear 3: Connect the Gears and Mine the Claim:**
Extended Value-Stream Improvement Implementation

Figure 7 *— The Engine Inside the System*

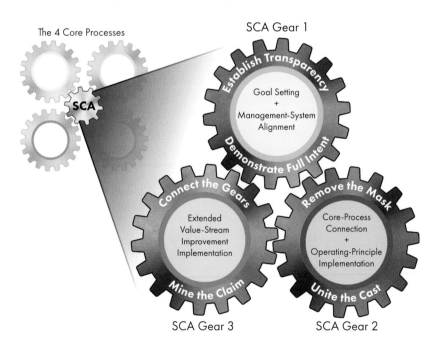

Supply-Chain Advancement connects the four core processes of the business.

1 SCA Gear 1: Establish Transparency and Demonstrate Full Intent:
Goal Setting + Management-System Alignment

Successful SCA requires the organization to be completely honest with itself relative to the current condition of supply-chain performance and the profit opportunity that is being missed because of a lack of advanced supply-chain performance. The CEO and senior leadership need to make a very formal declaration that hidden profit will be extracted from the business by connecting and integrating core business processes. This transparency of current and future state and commitment to the intent of SCA will allow the organization to set advanced supply-chain performance goals and establish a management system that leadership will embrace in order to achieve set goals to extract hidden profit. The core purpose of establishing transparency and demonstrating full intent is to set macro-level SCA goals and establish the management system that will ensure successful realization of set goals.

Figure 8 — *SCA Gear 1: SCA Goal Setting & Management-System Alignment*

Enabling Activities for SCA Gear 1
Goal Setting + Management-System Alignment

The first gear of the SCA machine is *Goal Setting and Management-System Alignment*. In this stage we will 1) set SCA macro-level goals, 2) teach and train our people, and 3) establish the SCA management system.

Gear 1 – Activity 1 | SCA Goals:
Vision–SCA Macro-Target Setting

Before we begin our work in SCA we need to understand what the prize is for completing the work. That is, how much profit is being left on the table because we do not have advanced supply-chain performance? Therefore, we need to understand thoroughly and objectively the current state, picture and articulate the ideal state, and use the current state/ideal state gap to set realistic yet challenging goals to be realized through SCA implementation.

Gear 1 – Activity 2 | SCA Education:
SCA Training and Education

While SCA is not complicated conceptually, operational realization will have its challenges because most leaders and organizations are very focused on optimization at the single-process or functional level. Therefore, integrating core processes and taking an extended value-stream approach to decision making will be new to most leaders. The best method to guide us through this change in management process is training and education. Leaders, managers, and all team members will need to understand the nature and purpose of SCA thinking, the benefits of advanced supply-chain performance, and the overall implementation strategy and tactical steps to be implemented.

Gear 1 – Activity 3 | Establishing Management System:
Management-System Design + Implementation

SCA implementation will succeed or fail based on the commitment to the management system established to support the initiative. The management system is the vehicle for executives to prove full intent to the work. The management system will set goals, guide the organization to make correct decisions, recognize deviations from plans, and bring visibility to initiate countermeasures quickly in order to achieve operational and strategic goals relative to SCA.

To complete this activity we will formalize the management infrastructure and leadership team to guide the implementation of SCA. We will confirm and align around the management system established and will develop the communication plan to show full SCA intent to the organization.

2 SCA Gear 2: Remove the Mask and Unite the Cast:
Core-Process Connection + SCA Operating-Principle Implementation

Many leaders wear masks that define them as their functional personalities and the roles their functions play in the overall staged production of the business. Consequently, the CEO has a cast of leaders that are focused on their own part of the production but not on the outcome of the production as a whole. No one is to blame for this situation as the management system of the business has created the masks and motivates cast members to be myopic in their view of the production. For successful SCA, we must remove the functional masks and unite the cast to focus on the success and outcome of the entire production across the entire script of the play.

Figure 9 — *SCA Gear 2: Core-Process Connection & SCA Operating-Principle Implementation*

Enabling Activities for SCA Gear 2
Core-Process Connection + SCA Operating-Principle Implementation

In this second gear of the SCA machine we will connect and integrate core business processes and sub-processes for successful realization of advanced supply-chain performance. This includes 1) developing and aligning on SCA operating principles, 2) choosing methods and tools to be implemented, and 3) setting process-level KPIs and business-improvement targets that will flow up to overall SCA goals and targets set in the first stage (Gear 1) of SCA. Last (4), we will develop and align on the overall roadmap and project-management approach to implementing SCA across the extended value stream of the organization.

The implementation of SCA operating principles is so critical that it makes up the entire second gear of SCA implementation.

Gear 2 – Activity 1 | SCA Core-Process Connection:
Operating-Principle Design + Alignment

This is a critical activity for SCA. In this step we develop, define, and formally align on the operating principles that will be implemented to realize SCA and achieve advanced supply-chain performance. The organization will develop the operating principles that will be used to connect and integrate the core processes of business strategy, product life-cycle management, sales and marketing, and supply-chain operations. The operating principles are the operations framework or guidelines that you believe to be the right strategy and set of tactics for SCA goals and results to be realized. The operating principles will guide the implementation of SCA and will create the bridges that allow core-process integration without wholesale restructuring of the organization.

Gear 2 – Activity 2 | Sub-Processes:
Sub-Process Identification + Operating Principles

Much of SCA business-improvement work will be accomplished at the sub-process level within the core processes of the business. (An example would be transportation being a sub-process of the core process of supply-chain operations.) Consequently, we need to identify these sub-processes and engage leaders and managers within these areas. In addition, SCA operating principles will need to be established within these sub-processes in order fully to connect and integrate the core processes of the business. In the next chapters we will roll out recommended sub-processes to be identified and chosen as key processes for SCA activities.

Gear 2 – Activity 3 | Methods and Tools: *Methods and Tools Development + Implementation*

Methods are the procedures, techniques, practices, or routines we will implement to integrate successfully SCA operating principles across the organization. Tools are the templates, technologies, visuals, and other tactical implements we will use to support the chosen methods. In the next chapters we will roll out recommended methods and tools to be embraced and implemented at the core-process level.

Gear 2 – Activity 4 | Measurement: *KPI Development + Target Setting*

Also a critical step for successful SCA, KPI and target setting must be completed at the operating-principle level. These measures will create the dashboard that will guide and instruct us relative to our progress in achieving overall goals set to extract hidden profit. These measures will also be integrated into the established management-system structure to support continued business improvement over the long term. In the next chapters we will roll out recommended KPIs and target focus areas to be embraced and implemented at the core-process level.

Gear 2 – Activity 5 | Business-Improvement Roadmap: *Extended Value-Stream Improvement Implementation*

The last step in Gear 2 is to plan, build, and integrate the roadmap to begin overall implementation of SCA. We will develop timelines, create risk-mitigation plans, and integrate the overall implementation roadmap into the established management-system structure. In this step we establish roles, responsibilities, and accountabilities and ensure that leadership is completely aligned around the SCA goals and objectives.

SCA Gear 3: Connect the Gears and Mine the Claim:
Extended Value-Stream Improvement Implementation

Discovering and extracting hidden profit is like mining for gold. You need to prospect, stake your claim, plan the work, and effectively execute to mine the gold, always having confidence the gold is there for the taking. The mining machine needs to be well oiled, and all of the gears need to work together across the entire claim. As we dig in search of the gold, we need to listen to the feedback of the digging and use this information to steer our course. We need to work hard, practice our new extended value-stream skills, experience trial and error, and recognize that the work may not always be easy but will always be rewarding.

Figure 10 — SCA Gear 3: Extended Value-Stream Improvement Implementation

Enabling Activities for SCA Gear 3
Extended Value-Stream Improvement Implementation

The last Gear in the SCA machine is to implement SCA and extract hidden profit by achieving advanced supply-chain performance. This will be an iterative process of *learn by doing* while leadership becomes more holistic in their view of the business. The key steps in this last gear are 1) managing to the Ten Rights across the extended value stream, 2) using supply-chain performance as a feedback loop, 3) instilling supply chain-centric decision making, 4) maturing our problem-solving capabilities across the organization, and 5) ultimately achieving SCA targets and re-aligning on new and more challenging SCA goals.

Gear 3 – Activity I | Ten Rights:
Ten Rights-Perspective Design + Implementation

This is the first step in leadership practicing and learning to be become holistic extended value-stream thinkers. We need to understand the extended value stream from the perspective of the Ten Rights across the entire business and not simply the last-mile delivery to the customer. In this step we design and map our supply-chain operations and network for SCA and develop supply chain-centric views to achieve *1) the right products, 2) to the right customers, 3) in the right quantities, 4) in the right quality, 5) at the right times, 6) from the right sources, 7) at the right prices, 8) at the right total cost, 9) with the right services, 10) all within the right amount of required complexity (effort)* across the extended value stream.

Gear 3 – Activity 2 | SC Feedback Loop:
Supply-Chain Performance Feedback-Loop Implementation

A fundamental axiom of SCA is that all value and waste created by any business decision will be manifested in the supply chain. Therefore, the supply chain is the reservoir of all intelligence relative to overall performance of business decisions made in the organization. SCA requires us to use supply-chain feedback as a barometer and indicating source for where we are creating customer value and where we are creating organizational waste. This feedback loop will be integrated into the established management-system structure and will be a primary driver for learning and prioritizing business-improvement initiatives.

Gear 3 – Activity 3 | SCC Decision Making:
Supply Chain-Centric Decision-Making Execution

Once we have implemented supply-chain performance as a feedback loop, we then need to create a culture where leadership takes anticipated supply-chain performance into consideration when making business decisions. This is logical based on the fact that the value and/or waste created by the decision will become evident in overall supply-chain performance. In this step we teach leaders to look at a business decision from the perspective of possible unintended consequences and unnecessary complexity that may be inadvertently injected into the supply chain as result of a business decision.

Gear 3 – Activity 4 | Problem Solving:
Process-Improvement Capability Evolution

All organizations want to improve the business; however, it is not a given that all people inside our organizations know how to solve problems formally. Solving problems exposed by SCA will require problem-solving skills, methods, and tools. The organization must also mature in its problem-solving focus and capabilities. This maturity progression will take the organization from 1) no formal problem solving to 2) functional problem solving to 3) core-process problem solving, and then to the ultimate SCA goal of 4) extended value-stream problem solving.

Gear 3 – Activity 5 | Goal Achievement:
Goal Setting + Management-System Alignment

SCA and Advanced Supply-Chain Performance are about achieving real, measured, and meaningful business results. This is about discovering and extracting hidden profit. Therefore, the last step of Gear 3 is to verify results and reconnect to Gear 1 to review performance, learn, and re-set and re-align around new goals and targets for the next period. This step shows the power and importance of the established management-system structure to continue to guide leadership, highlight gaps between plans vs. actual, prioritize, and decide what work will be undertaken in the short and long term.

Now that we have introduced SCA at a high level, we will use the next chapter to go into detail relative to Advanced Supply-Chain Performance and managing to the Ten Rights across the extended value stream.

From there, we will use the remainder of the book to detail the actions required to accomplish the three SCA focus areas of Establishing Transparency and Demonstrating Full Intent, Removing the Mask and Uniting the Cast, and Connecting the Gears and Mining the Claim.

Advanced Supply-Chain Performance

CHAPTER | 4

"…if the CEO is focused on supply-chain improvement, the company will be focused on it."

—ELIJAH RAY

dvanced Supply-Chain Performance is a major tenet of SCA. This is because supply-chain operations is the repository and last frontier for all decisions made within an organization. As already stated, no matter where a decision is made inside an organization, the value or waste created by that decision will eventually be manifested in the supply chain. Therefore, most business decisions made in all core processes of a business will affect supply-chain performance. A result of this is that supply-chain performance closely reflects overall business performance, and therefore feedback from supply-chain performance can be used as the foundation to determine business-improvement priorities. As well, and in contrast, supply-chain performance will also highlight where a lack of extended value-stream thinking is negatively affecting the business. Using this supply-chain performance feedback will drive visibility, alignment, and improvement within core business processes and will ultimately lead to more effective supply chain-centric decision making and overall improved business results.

In order to understand the impact SCA will have on *Advanced Supply-Chain Performance (ASCP)*, we first need to look at what we typically consider to be traditional supply-chain performance.

TRADITIONAL SUPPLY-CHAIN PERFORMANCE

The traditional way organizations describe supply-chain performance is by measuring whether they got *the right product to the right place in the right quantity at the right time and at the right logistics cost.* A qualitative description of this is *. . . Did we provide what the customer wanted when it was wanted in the desired quantity, and did we do all of this with minimal cost at the logistics functional level?* While these are important outcomes for any business, and they should not be ignored or eliminated as metrics, the problem with these traditional metrics of supply-chain performance is that they focus primarily on the last mile of order fulfillment. These metrics are simply outcome metrics and do not define the important business process drivers that ultimately lead to the outcome itself. Looking more closely, we see that our traditional views of supply-chain performance simply reflect our outbound and inbound logistics and manufacturing processes and not the overall combined or connected performance of all core processes within the business. Consequently, we ignore the fact that it is the combined effectiveness of core business processes that will drive the ultimate result for the customer and the business.

Traditional measures of supply-chain performance and focusing on the last delivery-mile outcome also have other significant weaknesses. These traditional measures fail to answer critical questions that we must address in order truly to understand overall business performance.

The most important questions traditional supply-chain performance views fail to answer are:

1. What was the overall lead time of the extended value stream in order to achieve this result?

2. How hard (effort/cost put forth) did the entire business have to work in order to achieve the result?

3. How does the result provide feedback to the business in order to connect upstream core business processes to define and improve upon the overall performance of the business?

4. Did we actually make profit delivering this product to this customer?

5. How many other products were simply sitting and waiting while we delivered this product?

Figure 11 — *Traditional Supply-Chain Performance*

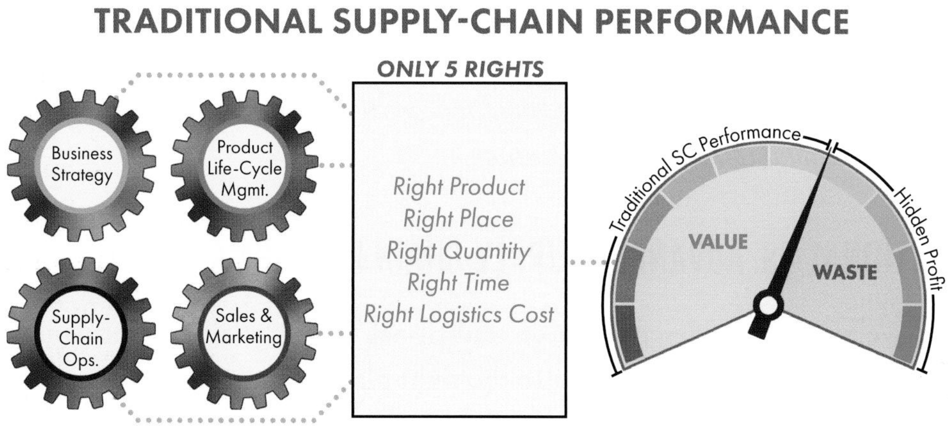

TRADITIONAL SUPPLY-CHAIN PERFORMANCE

ONLY 5 RIGHTS

Business Strategy

Product Life-Cycle Mgmt.

Supply-Chain Ops.

Sales & Marketing

Right Product
Right Place
Right Quantity
Right Time
Right Logistics Cost

Traditional SC Performance

VALUE

WASTE

Hidden Profit

Traditional Supply-Chain Performance only focuses on the last mile of delivery.

As we can see, traditional supply-chain performance metrics are effective in that they do measure the ultimate delivery to the customer (very important), and they do measure functional cost performance at the logistics level (transportation, warehousing, inventory turns). However, they do not provide measures or key performance indicators (KPIs) that clearly articulate the overall performance of the extended value stream or the combined and connected effectiveness of core processes within the business. The detrimental result of these traditional measures is that the organization does not produce feedback, data, or learning that will help to achieve Advanced Supply-Chain Performance (ASCP).

Consequently, to achieve *Advanced Supply-Chain Performance* it is imperative that we redefine how we describe supply-chain performance.

ADVANCED SUPPLY-CHAIN PERFORMANCE (ASCP)

The goal of Supply-Chain Advancement (SCA) is to produce *Advanced Supply-Chain Performance (ASCP)*. Ultimately this will produce superior results as defined by traditional supply-chain and business metrics in that we will more effectively deliver what the customer wants, when it is wanted, where it is wanted, and in the quantity wanted.

Continuing to build on our definition of Advanced Supply-Chain Performance, our definition now becomes:

Advanced Supply-Chain Performance is the measured incremental business performance we realize when we integrate and connect core business processes and implement supply chain-centric operating principles holistically to achieve the Ten Rights across the extended value stream of the organization in order to maximize customer value at the lowest possible total cost to the organization.

TRADITIONAL VS. ADVANCED SUPPLY-CHAIN PERFORMANCE

When we reviewed a description of traditional supply-chain performance, we described getting the right product to the right place at the right time in the right quantity and at the right cost. You will notice how these metrics have a single-process view and do not have an extended value-stream perspective or multiple connected-process view as they are focused on a particular event with a particular customer at a particular time and place. In contrast, the Ten Rights outlined in SCA for ASCP are in the plural form, recognizing they reflect the key metrics of extended value-stream performance.

Let's take a look at each of the Ten Rights of Advanced Supply-Chain Performance more closely.

ADVANCED SUPPLY-CHAIN PERFORMANCE | THE TEN RIGHTS

Right Products: Traditional supply-chain performance metrics measure whether we delivered a particular product that the customer requested for a particular order. Advanced Supply-Chain Performance (ASCP) follows the product theme across the extended value stream. With ASCP we ask whether we have the 1) right long-term product roadmap, 2) the right product mix, 3) the right product

Figure 12 — *Advanced Supply-Chain Performance*

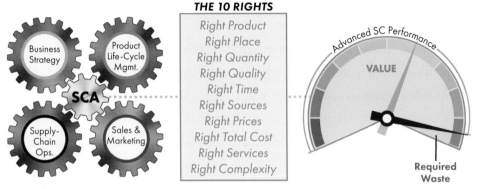

ADVANCED SUPPLY-CHAIN PERFORMANCE

Advanced Supply-Chain Performance connects the Four Core Processes and focuses on the 10 Rights across the Extended Value Stream.

differentiation, and 4) the right product variations across the extended value stream. SCA tells us that if we perform in these additional areas we will easily achieve getting the right product to a customer for a particular order (traditional metrics).

Right Customers (Place): Traditional supply-chain performance describes whether we shipped our product to the right customer location. ASCP goes beyond this and asks whether we have 1) the right targeted customer segments, 2) the right sales channels, and 3) the right end-to-end supply-chain system design, planning competency, and logistics infrastructure for the long term.

Right Quantities: Traditional supply-chain performance describes whether we shipped the right quantity of product as compared to the quantity the customer ordered for a discrete shipping event. ASCP looks at the quantities relative to the extended value stream. We describe ASCP as having 1) the right customer lot size and minimum order quantities, 2) the right finished-goods inventory-position quantities, 3) the right finished-goods replenishment quantities, 4) the right manufacturing-batch quantities, 5) the right raw-material inventory-position quantities, and 6) the right raw-material lot size and replenishment quantities. With ASCP, each of these quantity calculations is developed within the goals of minimizing overall extended value-stream lead times and reducing waste (inventory and logistics activities) in the end-to-end supply chain.

Right Quality: Traditional supply-chain performance metrics may not even take quality into consideration. When they do, it would typically be the key performance indicator of a mis-shipment, possibly product returns, or product recalls. At this point it is too late to use this information to improve business performance. Advanced Supply-Chain Performance (ASCP) looks at performance from the point of view of having 1) the right quality for purchase product sample, for engineering product sample, and for product production at each major stage (tollgate) in the extended value stream, 2) the right first-time-quality disciplines built into processes to identify and eliminate process errors and rework, and 3) the right cross-functional knowledge and skills for all team members in order to execute SCA and improve business performance.

Right Times: Traditional supply-chain performance describes whether we delivered our products to our customers at the right time (day, hour) the customer wanted to receive them. SCA looks at time from an End-to-End Supply-Chain Lead Time and Extended Value-Stream perspective.

From an Advanced Supply-Chain Performance (ASCP) point of view, time only consists of two variables, Value and Waste. In other words, all activities requiring time and effort are either adding value to our customer or they are not. Any time our processes or products are not having value added to them is considered waste. Therefore, it is logical to measure the effectiveness of our business by how long it takes us to create customer value through the extended value stream, including time spent on new-product creation.

With this in mind, from an SCA point of view, Advanced Supply-Chain Performance regarding the right times can be measured in two parts: Total Supply-Chain Operations Lead Time and the Extended Value-Stream Lead Time.

> *Total Supply-Chain Operations Lead Time = End-to-End Supply Chain =*
> *Inbound Supply-Chain Lead Time + Manufacturing Lead Time + Outbound*
> *Order-Fulfillment Lead Time*

A qualitative description of this would be, "If we received an order from our customer today, how long would it take us to order raw material from our suppliers, flow that material through our inbound supply chain, transform the material within our manufacturing process, and then ship the product to our customer as a finished good?"

Extended Value-Stream Lead Time = Time to Market =
Business Strategy Planning + Technology/Product-Creation Lead Time +
Production/Supply-Chain System Planning/Creation + Sales-Channel Planning/
Realization + Total Supply-Chain Operations Lead Time

Figure 13 — *The Components of End-to-End Supply-Chain Lead Time*

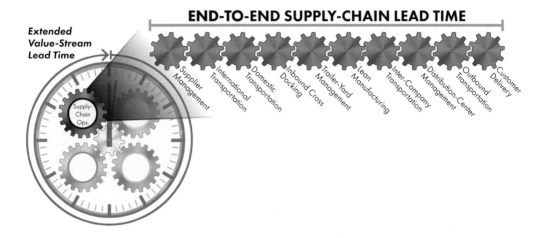

END-TO-END SUPPLY-CHAIN LEAD TIME

Extended Value-Stream Lead Time

Supply-Chain Ops.

Supplier Management · International Transportation · Domestic Transportation · Inbound Cross Docking · Trailer-Yard Management · Lean Manufacturing · Inter-Company Transportation · Distribution-Center Management · Outbound Transportation · Customer Delivery

End-to-End Supply-Chain Lead Time is only one component
of Extended Value-Stream Lead Time.

This overall lead time is a combined result of value and waste and therefore is an overall measure of Advanced Supply-Chain Performance. In addition, logic would support the argument that shorter lead times have less waste and more value in their overall equation. This is the fundamental reason why extended value-stream lead-time reduction is an operating principle of SCA.

Right Sources: Traditional supply-chain performance may not even take the right sources into consideration. Traditional decisions relative to sourcing may be made within product-development processes or procurement functions. Similarly, decisions relative to make vs. buy could be made within various business functions depending on the organization. In contrast, by connecting core business processes in order to make supply chain-centric decisions, SCA drives advanced performance by focusing on achieving the 1) the right supplier footprint, 2) the right delivery and supply agreements with the right suppliers for the long term, 3) the right manufacturing-location (including vertical integration) concepts relative to customer locations and cost structure, 4) the right logistics infrastructure design to support the right regions and sales channels based on overall customer service parameters, lead-time reduction, and optimizing total cost.

Right Prices: Traditional supply-chain performance would very rarely take the right pricing into consideration. Product pricing would typically be completed in product development or sales and marketing functions, which traditionally do not formally collaborate with supply-chain operations. Consequently, traditional supply-chain performance does not worry about product pricing, which is ironic and surprising when we consider that pricing is one of only two variables (cost is the other) that derive overall profit margin for an organization. ASCP drives visibility to ensure we have 1) the right customer-value propositions, 2) the right sales promotions, all resulting in 3) the right price to achieve the right profit in each region, sales channel, and customer and product category.

> Traditional supply-chain performance does not worry about product pricing, which is ironic and surprising when we consider that pricing is one of only two variables (cost is the other) that derive overall profit margin for an organization.

Right Total Cost: Traditional supply-chain performance would normally have metrics around cost. The challenge though is that these metrics would typically be logistics and supply-chain operations focused and would be focused on specific functions independently. Examples are traditional cost metrics around material cost, transportation costs, warehousing costs, and inventory turns, where an attempt is made to minimize each "cost bucket," and as a result the "extended value stream" is often sub-optimized.

ASCP drives total-cost thinking to achieve the right overall total system cost.

Total cost is the system-wide cost of a decision after all planned (required) and unplanned (not required) complexity is calculated into the cost of the decision. Total-cost thinking transcends functional divisional thinking and takes the extended value stream into account. This *whole* can include total material-sourcing cost, operating cost, lead-time costs, working-capital (inventory) costs, cost of poor quality, and cost of lost sales when making a decision. The goal of SCA is to reduce the total system-wide (extended value-stream) cost as opposed to reducing costs in silos at a functional level, which can result in sub-optimization and higher total costs. A quintessential example of total-cost thinking is understanding the total landed cost of a long-lead-time supplier when you take increased logistics and inventory cost into consideration as opposed to simply comparing one supplier piece price to another.

Total-cost thinking is not new to organizations conceptually, but many businesses are still unable to drive total-cost management across the organization. This is due to a lack of financial models and relevant data, lack of overall supply-chain financial knowledge, lack of total-systems thinking, and lack of alignment around operating principles within core business processes. SCA addresses these challenges through supply chain-centric decisions focused on reducing total cost of a system.

Figure 14 — *We Need to Become Total-Cost Thinkers*

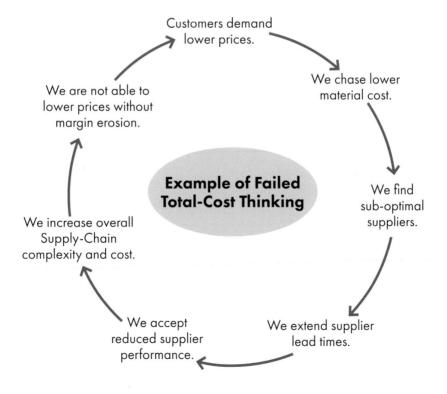

A lack of Total-Cost Thinking will lead to multiple unintended consequences and increased waste.

Right Services: Traditional supply-chain performance may not consider service requirements beyond the final delivery requirements. SCA and ASCP looks at service dynamics in the overall performance of supply-chain operations and the business. This includes ensuring we have 1) the right processes to make realistic and collaborative customer commitments, 2) the right competencies to provide service beyond the product itself, 3) the right knowledge, experience, and support to serve differing sales channels, markets, and customer needs, 4) the right processes and customer contacts to monitor voice of customer continually, 5) the right processes and management system to demonstrate that we are meeting and exceeding customer expectations.

Right Complexity (Effort): Traditional supply-chain performance would not generally factor extended value-stream complexity into the equation. Complexity in our businesses drives the essence of how hard we have to work to meet our goals. This focuses on the effort required to service the customer based on all of the required and non-required complexity we have introduced into the supply chain.

Overall effort is another SCA macro-measure of ASCP as we focus on having the right amount of required complexity. In other words, how hard do we need to work in order to generate a certain amount of customer satisfaction, revenue, and profit? This gets to the heart of complexity and associated waste and includes drivers such as: how many suppliers we have, how many raw material part numbers we require, what infrastructure (factories, transportation, and warehouses) we require, how many finished goods products (SKUs) we have, what inventory we need to hold, how hard that inventory works (turns), how many customers we need to service, and how many people we need in place to manage current supply-chain operations processes in their current state.

> **Complexity in our businesses drives the essence of how hard we have to work to meet our goals.**

SCA gives visibility to the effort we put forth in order to meet customer needs. Logically, we want to work towards generating more customer value, revenue, and profit with less effort (total cost) by reducing unnecessary complexity across the extended value stream.

Figure 15 — *The Ten Rights & Business Performance*

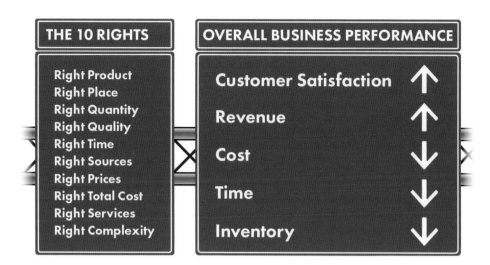

ADVANCED SUPPLY-CHAIN PERFORMANCE | OUTCOMES

As you can see, there is a fundamental and significant difference between traditional supply-chain performance definitions and the definition of Advanced Supply-Chain Performance as derived through the strategies of Supply-Chain Advancement.

In order to complete the story of Advanced Supply-Chain Performance, it's important to identify what overall business results we will achieve with respect to expected outcomes.

SCA is about real measured business results. This means we do expect to define overall supply-chain and business performance by outcome measures. These are:

Overall Business Improvement: Improved customer satisfaction, increased revenue, and improved margin by achieving the Ten Rights of Advanced Supply-Chain Performance across the extended value stream recognized by:

* increased revenue
* reduced operating cost
* reduced inventory
* reduced resources
* improved working capital

* improved return on assets
* reduced order-to-delivery lead time
* reduced cash-to-cash cycle
* improved first-time quality of processes
* continuous flow of product and information, creating visibility, transparency, and process stability throughout the organization

Notwithstanding this list of real business results, it is important to recognize that these are simply outcome measures. You cannot actually act upon these measures, but rather you achieve them when you accomplish the work and goals relative to SCA.

In that spirit, let's move on to understanding how we actually begin the implementation of Supply-Chain Advancement in order to achieve Advanced Supply-Chain Performance.

ACT 2

SCA
Implementation

Establish Transparency and Demonstrate Full Intent

CHAPTER | 5

> *"…if senior leaders have clearly communicated the company's strategic priorities throughout the organization, then managers and front-line employees can execute good, deliberate decisions around those tradeoffs."*

—HEATHER SHEEHAN

Transparency and demonstrating full intent are keystones to the successful change of our mental models and viewpoints on how to work within our organization. They also signal to employees that leaders are serious about accomplishing particular methods and goals being advocated.

Transparency can be described as *open and honest, not secretive, able to be seen through, easy to notice or understand.* Establishing transparency in an organization is about leaders and managers openly sharing the realities of operational performance regardless of the message we may be delivering.

Intent can described as *something you plan to do, an important goal you intend to achieve, a particular aim or purpose.* Demonstrating full intent is the communication tool that removes all doubt about the commitment to an initiative or strategy.

The following are details for SCA methodology for establishing transparency and demonstrating full intent.

1 SCA Gear 1: Establish Transparency and Demonstrate Full Intent:
Goal Setting + Management-System Alignment

The first gear in the SCA machine is to establish transparency and demonstrate full intent. The outcome of the first gear is to set our SCA macro-goals and design and implement the management system that will be used to ensure successful completion and long-term sustainment of the work.

Figure 16 — *SCA Gear 1: Goal Setting & Management-System Alignment*

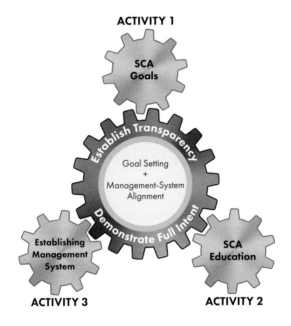

Enabling Activities for SCA Gear 1
Goal Setting + Management-System Alignment

* **Activity 1 | SCA Goals:** *Vision – SCA Macro-Target Setting*
* **Activity 2 | SCA Education:** *SCA Training and Education*
* **Activity 3 | Establishing Management System:** *Management-System Design + Implementation*

We will use the remainder of this chapter to outline the work and management methods to execute and implement these objectives effectively.

Gear I – Activity I | SCA Goals: *Vision–SCA Macro-Target Setting*

This first step is where we understand what the prize is for completing our work in SCA. We want to understand both thoroughly and objectively the current state, picture and articulate the ideal state, and use the current-state/ideal-state gap to set realistic yet challenging goals to be realized through SCA implementation. In the spirit of *first-time quality at the source,* this work is critical to the overall success of SCA as it brings visibility, transparency, and alignment around the realities of the current state of the business and the hidden profit that exists at a macro- or extended value-stream perspective.

The core purpose of this step is *to get the right people to agree on the right reality of the current state and design and agree upon the right vision of the ideal state* that will be realized with the implementation of SCA.

The two main bodies of work in this step are:

> **The goal of developing this team is to have the right leaders from the right processes aligned together with the right attitude and the right motivation to succeed with SCA.**

1. Determining the SCA team and implementation-management structure.
2. Setting SCA improvement goals.

SCA TEAM & IMPLEMENTATION-MANAGEMENT STRUCTURE

This first activity to implement SCA is to create the project-management structure inside the organization that will ensure complete support and commitment to the implementation strategy. It is very important for us to remember that SCA is not solely a supply-chain strategy; therefore SCA is not something that supply-chain executives implement on their own (although they would be great candidates to lead the effort).

SCA is a CEO-led initiative, and it requires board-level visibility and support. Consequently, we need to establish the implementation structure and team.

The goal of developing this team is to have the *right leaders* from the *right processes* aligned together with the *right attitude* and the *right motivation* to succeed with SCA.

The steps to accomplish this include:

1. **Sponsorship**: Board-level and CEO formal sponsorship is required.
2. **Project Leader:** One executive needs to be designated overall project leader, and this position requires straight-line accountability to the CEO and SCA board sponsor.
3. **Steering Committee:** SCA requires a steering committee that includes at least the senior leaders responsible for business strategy, product life-cycle management, sales and marketing, and supply-chain operations.
4. **SCA Team Members:** The overall team should include managers and employees from all four core business processes, thereby making up a horizontal representation of the extended value stream. *Note: As mentioned earlier, we do not want to discount the value of enabling processes: IT, HR, Safety, etc. Therefore it would beneficial and recommended that people from these areas be on the SCA team.*

Figure 17 — SCA Project Management

SCA PROJECT MANAGEMENT

The Supply-Chain Advancement project-management team is comprised of people from all levels of the organization.

Once this implementation structure is in place, we can move to setting SCA improvement goals.

SETTING SCA IMPROVEMENT GOALS

This stage of SCA is to set macro-level extended value-stream improvement targets and goals. This stage produces the overall explanation of *why we should do this work*. It is important to us as authors that we always remember that SCA is about achieving significant and measurable business results. Therefore, we need to identify and set targets relative to the hidden profit we intend to extract from current operations. These goals will then become the true north relative to what the organization expects to achieve with the important work associated with SCA.

This phase is critical because it establishes the overall vision of what we want to accomplish relative to our SCA goals. It is the first step in establishing extended value-stream perspective KPIs and setting improvement goals for the short and long term across core processes. In essence, this is the step where we understand how much impact we can have on the business by focusing on Advanced Supply-Chain Performance and business improvement across the extended value stream.

Below are four steps to set improvement goals that will be completed by the SCA team.

The goal of this phase of work is to have the *right picture of reality*, the *right vision (description) of the future,* and the *right plan of initiatives and extended value-stream KPIs* to realize the *right goals and targets* for extracting hidden profit through SCA.

> **The goal of this phase of work is to have the right picture of reality, the right vision (description) of the future, and the right plan of initiatives and extended value-stream KPIs to realize the right goals and targets for extracting hidden profit through SCA.**

1. **Current-State Analysis**: Analyze, map, and document current extended value-stream (connection of core processes) performance and identify current maturity relative to SCA principles and business-improvement capabilities.

2. **Ideal-State Analysis:** Introduce SCA operating principles and define and document the ideal (future) state relative to Advanced Supply-Chain Performance across the extended value stream using SCA operating principles as a catalyst for improvement ideas.

3. **Gap Analysis**: Complete a current-state/ideal-state gap analysis relative to SCA across the extended value stream. Calculate the business opportunities, both financial and operational, that are expected if we close the gap. List improvement initiatives required to achieve SCA and prioritize implementation order based on complexity of implementation and expected results for the business.

4. **Improvement Goal Setting:** Confirm, align upon, and commit to SCA Advanced Supply-Chain Performance goals to be used as targets in the short and long term. Develop executive-level extended value-stream KPI dashboards to be used in order to validate that real business results are being achieved within agreed-upon tollgates.

Figure 18 — Setting SCA Improvement Goals

SETTING SCA IMPROVEMENT GOALS

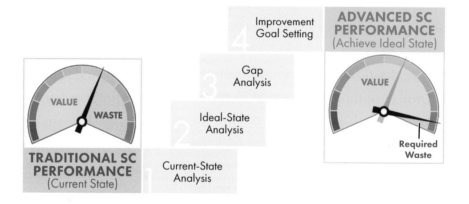

*Setting Supply-Chain Advancement Improvement Goals
is a structured and thoughtful process.*

Gear 1 – Activity 2 | SCA Education:
SCA Training and Education

An important action an organization can take to show team members respect is to train and educate and provide people with a vehicle to learn new skills to improve the value they bring to customers, the organization, and their own careers. Investing in people is also an ideal way to prove full intent to an initiative or corporate strategy.

SCA and extended value-stream thinking will be new for many organizations, as single-process and functionally focused cultures are well engrained in most companies. Asking people to pull up and view the extended value stream will certainly take people out of their comfort zone. In addition, SCA may appear to some people as the latest *program* that the organization is jamming down through the ranks.

Therefore, SCA training and education are critical so people 1) understand the concepts and operating principles of SCA, 2) believe in the goals and results that can be realized through SCA, 3) see and believe the SCA commitment made by leadership, 4) understand the work required for SCA and how it will affect their particular jobs, and 5) understand how SCA will positively affect the customer and the organization.

The purpose and goals of SCA training and education are to have the *right people* with the *right skills and tools* in the *right places* at the *right time* (ready to apply training) with the *right attitude* (believe in the vision) to work on the *right initiatives* all with the *right senior-level support.*

> **The purpose and goals of SCA training and education are to have the right people with the right skills and tools in the right places at the right time (ready to apply training) with the right attitude (believe in the vision) to work on the right initiatives all with the right senior-level support.**

SCA training and education can follow the following path of actions:

1. **Determine and Stratify Focus Groups:** SCA training and education (T&E) will require a different approach depending on the audience. By approach we mean curriculum modules, hours allocated to T&E, and expected outcomes of the training. All T&E should be focused on immediate application of the training upon completion, so curricula and action need to be tailored to people and process considerations.

   A first step in this stratification is to develop T&E engagements based on leadership level inside the organization, namely a T&E plan for: Executive Level, Senior Leaders, Mid-Level Managers, and Front-Line Team Members. After initial training is completed, we can then choose people to become Train-the-Trainer candidates.

2. **Create Development Path by Group:** Once we have determined our T&E focus groups we need to identify and plan the knowledge (curriculum) we want to transfer to each group. Curriculum will need to include transferring knowledge relative to SCA concepts, including but not limited to Extended Value-Stream Thinking, Connecting Core Processes through Supply Chain-Centric Decision Making, and Advanced Supply-Chain Performance.

In order to understand the level of training required, we need to know and plan around the current level of SCA concept knowledge within the organization. The steps to complete this activity are:

a. Create skills matrix for each group and each level (SCA Core-Competencies Matrix)
b. Assess current state by group
c. Analyze gap between current state and identified training needs (ideal state)
d. Develop curriculum (critical lessons) to support each working group's educational requirements
e. Develop delivery system for the training modules (classroom, on-the-job, on-line, self-study, project based)
f. Determine logistics and management-system support structure to ensure applied learning within training and education activities relative to overall SCA implementation goals
g. Execute training and verify applied learning and implementation of concepts

Upon completion of our planning and execution of training and education relative to SCA, we will need to ensure we have established the management system and structure to support, guide, and sustain SCA activities.

Gear 1 – Activity 3 | Establishing Management System: *Management-System Design + Implementation*

Establishing Management System

The success of SCA or any organizational improvement initiative rests in permanently embedding the elements of a structured improvement process into the management system. This is why SCA is so powerful, as SCA provides the necessary elements, such as goal setting, operating principles, extended value-stream key-performance indicators, and review tollgates to be incorporated into the management system based on feedback from overall supply-chain performance.

The purpose of designing and establishing the SCA management system is to ensure successful SCA implementation by ensuring the *right people* are having the *right conversations* about the *right measures* at the r*ight time and place* to uncover the *right problems* and collectively determine the *right targets and solution*s to be implemented to close gaps relative to plan vs. actual conditions.

An organizational management system is the aggregate, or sum, of all of the processes designed to enable leaders to set goals, guide the organization, make correct decisions, recognize deviations from plans, and initiate honest conversations leading to countermeasures quickly in order to achieve operational and strategic goals.

All organizations have management systems, some formal and others informal, all with varying degrees of rigor. However, most lack an overall extended value-stream approach for focused and connected core-process business improvement.

It is absolutely critical to realize that any significant improvement initiative within an organization will live or die depending on the rigor and leadership commitment to the supporting management system. SCA will develop the management-system structure to navigate SCA through required annual and quarterly strategic reviews of SCA results, monthly and weekly tactical reviews of advanced supply-chain performance, and daily and hourly reviews of process performance.

> **An organizational management system is the aggregate, or sum, of all of the processes designed to enable leaders to set goals, guide the organization, make correct decisions, recognize deviations from plans, and initiate honest conversations leading to countermeasures quickly in order to achieve operational and strategic goals.**

The steps to establish the management system for successful SCA are:

1. **Establish Roles and Responsibility:** Define/Refine the roles and responsibilities of all leaders of business core processes to drive continued alignment and commitment to the implementation of SCA operating principles, set goals, and supply chain-centric decision making.

2. **Review Structure**: Develop and implement a formal meeting and status-report (conversational update) structure with standardized key performance indicators and templates to assess plan versus actual condition, to bring visibility to gaps, to understand root causes of gaps, and successfully to develop and implement countermeasures to ensure planned SCA goals are realized. It is critical in this phase that we not only review extended value-stream KPIs but also have content discussion *around how we reached this KPI and what we learned.*

   Note: *Going to the actual place of value creation (Go See) may be critical for these conversations to be honest, transparent, and fact based.*

3. **Deploy Short-Term Goals**: Determine, verify, set, and gain vertical and cross-functional leadership alignment around measurable, realistic yet challenging goals and objectives relative to SCA for the next review period. Ensure these short-term goals flow up to the overall SCA roadmap and KPIs. Implement the targets within the SCA operating principles for all core processes and sub-processes to guide supply chain-centric decision making across the extended value stream.

4. **Learn Lessons:** From the review and tollgate process, capture lessons learned and build these lessons into future organizational development, goal setting, and execution activities. Embed these improvements into the management system and goal-setting process.

The above list of activities completes the initiatives within our first gear of SCA. We will now move to SCA Gear 2 – Removing the Mask and Uniting the Cast.

Remove the Mask and Unite the Cast

CHAPTER | 6

> *"...I once looked at the goals and bonuses of every functional head of our company: manufacturing, procurement, marketing, sales, and logistics. They were clearly in conflict."*
>
> —RICK D. BLASGEN

Organizations are often successful in spite of themselves. Taken to an extreme, we have witnessed cultures where leaders purposely do not collaborate across core processes; performance measures and rewards systems are single process or function focused and sometimes gamed and manipulated; KPI performances tell a story that is disconnected from actual business results (including customer satisfaction); and leaders who excel at this art full time are often those in good standing and may even receive the best promotions.

In spite of all this, the organization may still produce results that are acceptable to shareholders, while customers are certainly negatively affected and employees simply punch their clock in complete dismay over leadership and the organization in general. In the end, it would appear that many leaders are simply playing a masked role in a "play" that has multiple versions of scripts across the organization.

Note: If you are an organization that is profitable in spite of disconnected processes, just think about how profitable you could be. Always remember, traditional performance is the enemy of advanced performance.

We understand that the above scenario is a very negative picture and perhaps extreme, but our experience would suggest that we are at times not far off the mark. The purpose of SCA is to remove the masks that exist inside our organizations in order to produce complete and honest transparency relative to uncovering and extracting hidden profit. This is a critical juncture for leaders, as SCA will not succeed if leadership is not committed to honest and open transparency. In order for SCA to succeed, we can no longer accept the notion that *Bad is Good* and we need to measure, articulate, and report outcomes as they truly are, regardless of how challenging the reality is. Once accomplished with corporate sincerity, this can be a very *freeing* outcome for leadership, and you can be certain that employees at all levels of the organization will be appreciative, as most of the team knows the harsh reality anyway.

The metaphor of *Remove the Mask and Unite the Cast* is well intended to exemplify that we are all cast members in the same play, although it may seem at times that we do not read from the same script. If we were to examine and describe these masks relative to the core processes, what might it look like?

THE MASKS OF THE FOUR CORE PROCESSES

* **Business Strategy** has the mask of confidence and unknown challenge, as we dream of what is possible, often without the use of supporting data for the future or a true understanding of our current strengths and weaknesses.
* **Product Life-Cycle Management** has the mask of creativity and control, with absolute belief that we fully understand the customers and can create what they desire, often without knowledge of the real value or additional complexity we add to the business.
* **Sales and Marketing** has the mask of agreement and optimism as we believe we can deliver upon any promise made to the customer, often with total disregard of actual operational capabilities of the business.

> * **Supply-Chain Operations** has the mask of concern, worry, and anxiety, as we know the extent of our true capabilities and wonder what the blind impact will be with respect to the implications of confidence, challenge, creativity, control, agreement, and optimism of the preceding core processes.

Figure 19 — *Masks of the Four Core Processes*

BUSINESS STRATEGY	PRODUCT LIFE-CYCLE MGMT.	SALES & MARKETING	SUPPLY-CHAIN OPERATIONS
Great Confidence	Abundant Creativity	Vulnerable Optimism	Realistic Concern
Endless Possibilities	Control of Destiny	Ready to Commit	Functional Isolation
Unknown Challenges	Unknown Consequences	Unknown Capabilities	Known Probable Outcomes

With these masks representing our core processes, we act out the play reading from different scripts, and then we are often surprised when the ending is not what we expected. SCA and the implementation of supply chain-centric operating principles will remove these masks and enable us to read from one script, consequently uniting the cast to create, develop, act out, and achieve the ending we desire.

Here is what is most important though. The above current state in most organizations is not a result of dishonest or unqualified leaders. The current condition is a result of functionally focused management systems (with poor KPIs) and corporate institutions that are not focused on connecting core processes or improving the extended value stream through the implementation of supply chain-centric operating principles. *This goes far beyond the old saying of* **you get what you measure** *and describes the environment more accurately as* **you get what you collaboratively believe in and act upon***!*

The essence of SCA is operating principles and *what you believe in*, so let's begin to roll out exactly what it is we need to believe in collaboratively.

2 SCA Gear 2: Remove the Mask and Unite the Cast:
Core-Process Connection + SCA Operating-Principle Implementation

The overall purpose of our second gear is to have the *right leaders* aligned and committed to the r*ight operating principles* to connect the *right core processes* and the *right sub-processes*. These operating principles will drive the *right methods*, the *right tools,* and the *right KPIs* to achieve the *right business improvement* across the extended enterprise.

Figure 20 — *SCA Gear 2: Core-Process Connection & SCA Operating-Principle Implementation*

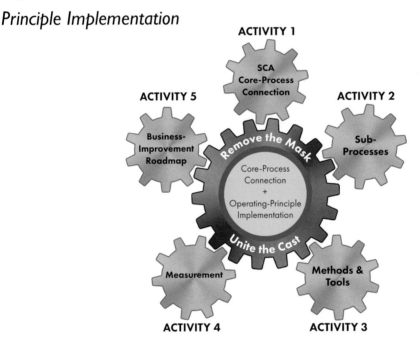

Enabling Activities for SCA Gear 2
Core-Process Connection + SCA Operating-Principle Implementation

* **Activity 1 | SCA Core-Process Connection:** *Operating-Principle Design + Alignment*
* **Activity 2 | Sub-Processes:** *Sub-Process Identification + Operating Principles*

* **Activity 3 | Methods and Tools:** *Methods and Tools Development + Implementation*
* **Activity 4 | Measurement:** *KPI Development + Target Setting*
* **Activity 5 | Business-Improvement Roadmap:** *Extended Value-Stream Improvement Implementation*

This second SCA Gear is critical to our SCA initiative. This is where we truly decide and align on our corporate belief system relative to how we will lead and manage the extended value stream.

In the following chapters we will explore the details of these activities relative to each core process, namely, Business Strategy, Product Life-Cycle Management, Sales and Marketing, and Supply-Chain Operations.

To complete this chapter, we will further discuss the importance and implementation steps of SCA Operating Principles, and we will introduce the Operating Principles recommended for each SCA Core Process.

OPERATING-PRINCIPLE DESIGN + ALIGNMENT | GETTING STARTED

Below are the high-level implementation steps to prepare for the implementation of SCA operating principles:

1. **Define and Align on Operating Principles:** Develop and finalize the list of core-process operating principles to be embraced, and then ensure complete alignment within the SCA steering committee.

2. **Tools and Methods:** Beginning with the finalized list of operating principles, develop the vision for operational tools and management methods to be used in order to operationalize the operating principles within the extended value stream.

3. **KPI – Target Development:** Beginning with the finalized list of operating principles, define key performance indicators (KPIs) and build a KPI dashboard to be used as measures within the established implementation-management system. These extended-value stream KPIs will describe Advanced Supply-Chain Performance for each operating principle and build into the macro-KPIs being used to define success for the overall SCA implementation. *Note: We will delve into details relative to SCA KPIs in chapter 11.*

4. **Socialization and Implementation Planning**: Connecting to the training and education in Gear 1, we need to socialize SCA operating principles, communicate the vision and roadmap and all planning for the implementation of the operating principles. Last, we need to create the project-management tools to support the implementation of operating principles.

Figure 21 — Operating-Principle Implementation Steps

A common definition of the word principle is *fundamental truth or mental paradigm that serves as the foundation for a system of belief or behavior or for a chain of reasoning*. More simply put, a principle is something you steadfastly believe in. This belief is absolute and is built upon a foundation based on your education, industry best practices, experience, and what you have learned as a leader and professional. Therefore, an Operating Principle is an operations framework or guideline that you believe is the right strategy or tactic for goals and results to be realized. Operating principles are critical in today's complex business environment as they guide leadership and employee behavior, decision making, selection of methods and tools to operationalize the principles, measure progress, and ultimately determine whether leadership within an organization is aligned on how goals will be achieved. SCA is based on implementing specific operating principles within core business processes across the extended value stream.

Operating principles reflect leadership priorities and guide the design and management of business processes. Therefore, they are critical for setting direction and deciding what work we will actually perform. The absence of operating principles will result in frequent changes of strategy and tactics and will only serve to confuse and frustrate the organization.

It is important not to confuse corporate values with operating principles. For example, *integrity* may be an organizational value, where a belief system around *lead-time reduction* would be considered an operating principle. When developing operating principles effectively, it is important to understand the actual work that is required in order to operationalize the operating principles as it is the need for leadership alignment around the work that actually creates extended value-stream thinking. Completing our example of lead-time reduction, the work would include supplier and manufacturing-location selection, material lot-size management, manufacturing-batch sizing and customer delivery-frequency planning. To accomplish this work effectively will require alignment and collaboration among all four core business processes relative to lead-time reduction as an operating principle. In contrast, if we are not aligned around the operating principle, decisions may be made within the four core processes that will contradict each other, be sub-optimal, and probably actually increase lead time and ultimately create waste in the supply chain.

SCA is based on implementing specific operating principles within core business processes across the extended value stream.

SCA FOUR CORE-PROCESS OPERATING PRINCIPLES

For SCA purposes, the four core processes we need to connect are **Business Strategy, Product Life-Cycle Management, Sales and Marketing, and Supply-Chain Operations.** By *connect* we mean that the core processes are integrated and act as one system, where we make supply chain-centric decisions that result in flow and advanced supply-chain performance and not in unplanned complexity and associated waste. This is not about a reorganization of the organizational structure, but rather this is recognition that each core process is a gear in the *business machine* and that the gears need to connect with each other for the *machine* to be effective.

SCA Operating Principles are the main management method to connect these core processes. The following is a list of recommended SCA Operating Principles that are connected to a particular core process. Please beware that you will have a strong propensity to say *that does not belong there* or *we do that over here!* And this is exactly the point. These operating principles will require cross-functional collaboration to be implemented successfully. Our allocation of a principle to a particular core process is a recommendation on which core process should take the lead in implementing the operating principle across the extended value stream, fully recognizing it will require highly collaborative and participatory management to be successful.

SCA FOUR CORE-PROCESS OPERATING PRINCIPLES

1. **Business Strategy | SCA as a Differentiating Competency:** SCA and resulting Advanced Supply-Chain Performance are an organizational core competency and strategic market differentiator.

2. **Product Life-Cycle Management | Long-Term Collaborative Product Planning:** Long-term product and sales-channel roadmaps are created collaboratively with simultaneous development of supporting material sourcing, manufacturing, and distribution-planning roadmaps.

3. **Sales and Marketing | Collaborative Demand and Profit Planning:** Highly collaborative customer demand, production, and material planning with a goal of stable and profitable sales growth.

4. **Supply-Chain Operations | Reliable Delivery + Speed and Visible Flow:** Highly reliable delivery and capable speed with end-to-end supply-chain visibility focuses on implementing and controlling leveled flow and velocity across an extremely stable and reliable logistics network.

IMPLEMENTING SCA FOUR CORE-PROCESS OPERATING PRINCIPLES

We will use the next chapters to go into detail about the SCA Operating Principles for each of these core processes. In particular, we will answer:

* What is the purpose of the core process in general, and in particular what is the purpose of the core process relative to SCA?
* What are current problems that exist with this core process, and consequently what is the ideal state for this process relative to SCA?
* What are the operating-principle commitments that need to be implemented within the core process to achieve advanced supply-chain performance?
* What critical sub-processes should also be grouped into SCA initiatives for development of extended value-stream operating principles for the particular sub-process?

* What management systems, methods, and tools are available to help with implementation of the operating principles?
* What extended value-stream KPIs should we use to measure the success of the operating principles for Advanced Supply-Chain Performance?

Figure 22 — *SCA Four Core-Process Operating Principles*

We will take a focused perspective on each core-process operating principle to go through these activities. This will allow us to understand better the current condition and ideal SCA condition of the specific core process as well as the plan for implementation of the recommended SCA core-process operating principle. This planning for implementation includes understanding what specific sub-processes we should act upon, what tools and methods we can deploy, and what extended value-stream targets and metrics (KPIs) we should focus on to articulate and validate measurable results.

The goal is to implement the right methods, tools, and metrics to accomplish our SCA goal of connecting core processes to drive extended value-stream thinking and achieve advanced supply-chain performance.

The situation may arise that recommendations, in particular KPIs, may conflict with current approaches. This is good news, as there is a high probability that current methods and measures may in fact be driving functional behaviors that are contradictory to SCA. This realization is the catalyst for a new and constructive dialogue relative to current methods and performance-management systems. In fact, our work and experience to date actually allow us to conclude that ineffective management methods and KPIs may be the most damaging variable leading to failed attempts for long-term business improvements.

Consequently, as we go through the next several sub-chapters on the core processes, it is beneficial and in many cases critical to be comparing SCA methods with established cultural elements of your organization's current state. Once again, all gaps identified are good news, as these gaps provide the path for discovering hidden profit.

SCA as a Differentiating Competency

CHAPTER | 7

SCA Operating Principle

"…bringing functional groups together to work effectively starts with having compelling business reasons for change."

—RICK SATHER

Business Strategy is the core process that develops and sets the course for the business derived from the mission, vision, values, and extensive market and customer research. From a tactical point of view, this involves the development of customer-value propositions, business-growth strategies, setting of market and financial goals, and development of the core competencies required to support the strategy. In the end, business strategy will span all business functions to identify how the company best competes and adapts to market conditions in order to remain relevant and competitive.

From a Supply-Chain Advancement (SCA) perspective, within the business strategy process we are focused on identifying preferred targeted product/services, customer segmentation, and geographical-region market development. These particular focus areas are important because they will ultimately have significant implications on overall supply-chain network design that will provide feedback to the organization in order to facilitate both an understanding of the implications of past decisions and prioritizing business-improvement opportunities.

Secondly, relative to SCA, business strategy also determines the level of supply-chain competency, supply-chain competitiveness, and supply-chain strategy sustainability (rigor) we are going to pursue. This means that our commitment to advanced supply-chain performance will be determined within the core process of business-strategy development.

BUSINESS STRATEGY | CURRENT-STATE PROBLEMS RELATIVE TO SCA

Relative to SCA, business strategy often lacks deep analysis or knowledge of customer needs, market information, and competitive intelligence reaching far enough into the future. This can lead to misguided conclusions. Therefore, strategies at times are based on facts derived from various high-level studies and analysis and are also significantly based on assumptions made by leaders from their own functional viewpoint. The validity of these assumptions may not be sufficiently tested and often can be wrong, leading to late changes in product design, failed marketing initiatives, reduced market penetration, and significant changes in supply-chain requirements and overall supply-chain design.

> **Business strategy also determines the level of supply-chain competency, supply-chain competitiveness, and supply-chain strategy sustainability (rigor) we are going to pursue.**

In these situations, the strategy does not produce a clear path of actionable steps on how to compete. The resulting plan to implement the strategy will not be specific enough or sufficiently future oriented and will be subject to frequent changes, resulting in organizational confusion, unplanned complexity, and waste in the supply chain as a result of decisions made in other parts of the business.

Secondly, business strategy can be too broad regarding the product and markets to be served, and often our strategy may be communicated to the customer too early and without thorough evaluation. The resulting commitments to our customers may not be fulfilled by the different functions or the current supply-chain system design. This is due to the fact that the business strategy lacks clarity on what flexibility is needed over time from supply-chain operations, and this ultimately causes unplanned and costly supply-chain system re-designs over the product life cycle. Yet all of this is simply a result of a lack of extended value-stream thinking; our supply-chain functions are not sufficiently involved in the strategy-development process; and supply chain-relevant concerns are not addressed proactively. As a result of this lack of extended value-stream approach, supply-chain network design will be based on insufficient design criteria resulting in unnecessary complexity and waste and will not reach an advanced supply-chain performance level.

Finally, possibly the most serious problem that exists today is that organizations view supply-chain operations solely as a cost center, an evil cost of doing business that you simply have to put up with. Taken to extremes, the organization will blindly strive to outsource supply-chain and logistics processes, losing control of extended value-stream business-improvement activities. This is not to suggest that third parties cannot play a role in supply-chain strategy; however, the reason for outsourcing cannot simply be an expectation of cost reduction. There must be a value proposition relative to outsourced partners beyond cost, and we need to maintain the expertise, visibility, and control of all supply-chain operations across the entire network. In other words, even when we outsource supply-chain and logistics processes, we need to remain in control and lead the management system that drives business improvement.

> **Within SCA, an organization will view the supply chain as a lever for profitability in top-line revenue growth, reduced operation costs, improved working capital, and margin improvement.**

Within SCA, an organization will view the supply chain as a lever for profitability in top-line revenue growth, reduced operation costs, improved working capital, and margin improvement. This is accomplished by implementing a business strategy that drives extended value-stream management and supply-chain operations as a competitive weapon and overall strategic differentiator. It is imperative that a business recognize it must have supply-chain competencies in order to achieve long-term business improvement.

BUSINESS STRATEGY | IDEAL STATE RELATIVE TO SCA

In our SCA ideal state, the organization views SCA and extended value-stream management as a strategic priority. Business strategy will consult, develop, align around, and drive detailed actionable steps in order to implement a sustainable supply-chain strategy that will leverage supply-chain operations as a core competency, competitive weapon, and market differentiator. Consequently, the SCA operating principle for business strategy is *SCA as a Differentiating Competency*.

SCA OPERATING PRINCIPLE
BUSINESS STRATEGY

The SCA operating principle for Business Strategy is:

<u>SCA as a Differentiating Competency</u>: SCA and resulting Advanced Supply-Chain Performance are an organizational core competency and strategic market differentiator.

Commitment: The organization is committed to SCA capability and developing SCA into a core competency and clear differentiator in the marketplace. The strategic commitment is to use supply-chain feedback continuously to prioritize business-improvement initiatives and to have absolute discipline to improve towards maximizing customer value at the lowest possible total cost across the extended value stream.

BUSINESS STRATEGY | SCA SUB-PROCESSES

As we implement SCA, the actual work we need to complete will involve sub-processes within the organization. Relative to SCA and business strategy, these sub-processes will include: Strategy-Planning Process, Customer-Value Planning, Supply-Chain Technology Planning, Sales Market + Region-Planning Process, and Supply-Chain Organizational-Capability Planning Process.

Note: We recognize this is not an exhaustive list of sub-processes, and the terms may not be those used in all organizations. The key point here is that SCA, extended value-stream management, and supply chain-centric decision making will require dialogue, commitment, and actionable steps to be taken within sub-processes of the organization. As we mature in our SCA thinking, we will develop operating principles within these sub-processes of the company.

BUSINESS STRATEGY | SCA METHODS AND TOOLS

The following are a list of methods or tools that are recommended for implementing SCA and the SCA operating principle for Business Strategy.

1. **Market, Product, and Competitor Analysis:** Complete yearly core-process (Product Life-Cycle, Sales and Marketing, Supply-Chain Operations) and strategy-planning process including SWOT, mega-trend analysis, product-market analysis, and competitor-product analysis supported by a product/after-purchase service-planning process.

    The goal is to validate that we have the right products being developed and sold to the right customers in the right places with the right complexity (value) and right service.

2. **Extended Value-Stream Mapping:** Complete a full extended value-stream map, including product development, sales and marketing, and supply-chain operations. Focus on one particular product from product-concept development to first-customer delivery of the product. The map will identify: total extended value-stream lead time, core-process decision-making connection points (disconnects that create waste), first-time quality (errors that result in re-work), and an analysis of decision making relative to each of the Ten Rights.

    The goal is to create alignment relative to the current state and ideal state relative to connecting the core processes of the business and to set targets for the market-relevant total extended value-stream lead time (time to market). Secondly, we identify and implement overall improvement plans for supply chain-centric decision making relative to achieving the Ten Rights.

3. **Advanced Supply-Chain Performance Analysis:** Building on the first two activities above, we identify and create visibility of the gap between our current supply-chain performance and the performance we will achieve when we connect the core processes of the business. This allows us to quantify the value that advanced supply-chain performance will bring to the organization in order for us to make SCA implementation decisions about resources, time,

and investment. Identifying the supply-chain performance gap will identify operational and financial opportunities and itemize and prioritize initiatives (SCA improvement projects) based on ease of implementation and positive impact on the business. This work includes analysis of current and ideal state relative to the Ten Rights and outcome measures including revenue, supply-chain operating costs, working capital (inventory), and end-to-end supply-chain lead time (raw material to manufacturing to customer delivery).

The goal is to have the right targets and the right priorities of planned initiatives to achieve advanced supply-chain performance.

4. **Supply-Chain Competency Analysis:** Complete and document competitiveness and supply-chain competency analysis and align around the desired balanced approach to goals relative to speed, cost, quality, delivery, customer intimacy, and innovation. Understand the current condition and desired condition relative to people, process, and technology needs in supply-chain operations, completing make-versus-buy analysis (outsource) for supply-chain operational processes. Use roles and responsibilities and skills matrices to determine gaps that exist in people skills and knowledge relative to SCA and supply-chain management expertise.

The goal is to execute the right plan for the right level of supply-chain operations competency.

Figure 23 — *Business Strategy Steps*

BUSINESS STRATEGY | SUMMARY

Implemented effectively, **<u>SCA as a Differentiating Competency</u>** will produce the:

* right collaboration across the extended value stream;
* right extended value-stream network design;
* right responsiveness to customer demands;
* right visibility of customer and market needs;
* right flexibility and adaptability to market change;
* right overall complexity and right total cost; and
* right profit with the right effort.

Long-Term Collaborative Product Planning

CHAPTER | 8

SCA Operating Principle

"…decisions late in the product life-cycle and stage-gate process negate a lot of work that's already done."

—SUE ARMSTRONG

Product and Service Life-Cycle planning and management includes the inception of a product or service, product design and engineering, planning for material sourcing, planning for manufacturing, planning for distribution, value-added services, and ultimate product retirement or disposal. Product life-cycle management is an interesting core process in that many organizations have the process structured differently and with varying degrees of responsibilities and accountabilities as described above. For example, not all product life-cycle functions drive planning for inbound logistics, manufacturing, or outbound distribution. Or if they do, they do so without collaborating across the organization, or they do so without content knowledge of the supply-chain operations they are planning. This is one of our main challenges and therefore is a significant SCA opportunity.

Relative to SCA, we need to expand the role and function of Product Life-Cycle Planning processes, and we need to connect this role with the other three core

> **The main issues that exist today in product life-cycle management and planning are with incomplete product-planning roadmaps, unplanned complexity, and a lack of supply-chain operations knowledge within the product-planning function.**

processes to create our extended value-stream perspective. For example, during product life-cycle planning we need to ensure that competitive and differentiating products are defined, required product variations over the product life cycle are determined, customer services beyond delivering the product are identified, raw material sources are determined (including make-versus-buy decisions), manufacturing processes and manufacturing locations are determined, and the overall logistics system (network) from supplier to manufacturing to the customer is designed and planned to support targeted sales channels.

The powerful aspect of this up-front *extended value-stream* viewpoint is that this work cannot be accomplished in a functional silo. Leaders from all core functions will be required to collaborate in order to accomplish this goal. Consequently, and as we will see, connecting Product Life-Cycle Management to the rest of the organization is critical for successful SCA.

PRODUCT LIFE-CYCLE MANAGEMENT | CURRENT-STATE PROBLEMS RELATIVE TO SCA

The main issues that exist today in product life-cycle management and planning are with incomplete product-planning roadmaps, unplanned complexity, and a lack of supply-chain operations knowledge within the product-planning function. Innovation and product-selection processes often lack a long-term product roadmap with planned differentiation and planned product complexity. This will result in unstable product plans and frequent reactive product changes, causing unnecessary complexity in operations (all parts of the extended value stream) and waste in the supply chain.

One challenge is that product variations are often excessive, without significant differentiation or customer value being created by the unnecessary complexity. The implication for operations and the supply chain resulting from the product-variation requirements (shape, color, function, packaging, etc.) are grossly underestimated and lead to significant waste in manufacturing and logistics processes, as well as increased lead time, increased inventory (waste of overproduction), and reduced overall supply-chain performance. As noted in the beginning of this book, in many cases this new level of complexity has exceeded our process and people knowledge capabilities for managing the complexity without excessive costs to the business.

Building upon current challenges, customer services beyond the delivery of a product are often not proactively planned. The organization will be in a reactive mode to customer service requests without thorough evaluation, which can lead to unprofitable service agreements. These types of unplanned services often disrupt supply-chain processes, causing more unnecessary complexity and cost burden. Hence the typical *fire-fighting* culture.

Moving into supply-chain operations processes, often supplier (material/service) sourcing and planning is not focused long term and does not consider growth of the product in different markets and regions. Therefore we don't consider or determine the correct manufacturing and supplier footprint. This creates a suboptimal supply-chain design leading to unnecessary complexity, risk, and cost in the supply chain. This complexity will manifest itself in excessive replenishment times, dependency on single sources, currency exchange-rate risks, limited purchasing power, extended lead times, and excessive inventory, not to mention failure to service our factories and customers.

In addition, manufacturing planning may not be based on the most likely long-term product life-cycle changes and volume scenarios. Intelligence for a realistic volume ramp-up can be insufficient, resulting in manufacturing systems that lack suitable levels of automation, required flexibility for product mix (where product changes are not planned), or simply insufficient capacity to meet actual customer demands. In these cases, logistics and supply-chain operations planning will lack knowledge of all variables during the product life cycle, such as volume scenarios, product variations, manufacturing-location selection, supplier locations, customer locations or service offerings, and commitments made to

> **One challenge is that product variations are often excessive, without significant differentiation or customer value being created by the unnecessary complexity.**

customers. All of this results in supply-chain operations that are not connected or integrated with product life-cycle management processes, resulting in increased complexity, excessive lead times, excessive inventories, reactive firefighting at the tactical level, and higher overall total cost to the organization, all while potentially missing out on revenue opportunities.

As we can see, there is an enormous amount of value that can be unlocked when we connect product life-cycle planning and management to the rest of the business and manage the system from an extended value-stream point of view.

PRODUCT LIFE-CYCLE MANAGEMENT | IDEAL STATE RELATIVE TO SCA

Relative to SCA, product life-cycle management incorporates long-term product-roadmap planning with a focus on stability and predictability in terms of product features, product variations, markets, and sales channels served. Product-volume scenarios need to be realistic and connected to targeted sales channels so we can proactively design the supply chain for manufacturing and supply-chain operations capabilities and flexibilities. Supply-Chain Network design, including inbound sourcing, manufacturing, and outbound distribution, is highly flexible and reliable, and replenishment processes are based on customer consumption acting as the pace-setting process. Customer service beyond the product is well planned and does not disrupt day-to-day operations unexpectedly, while disciplined product retirement processes are in place and executed as effectively as new-product introduction.

> **Customer service beyond the product is well planned and does not disrupt day-to-day operations unexpectedly, while disciplined product retirement processes are in place and executed as effectively as new-product introduction.**

The goal of product life-cycle management should not be simply to introduce new products, but rather to introduce new products that will be highly profitable because they produce maximum customer value at the lowest possible complexity and lowest total cost to the organization.

SCA OPERATING PRINCIPLE
PRODUCT LIFE-CYCLE MANAGEMENT

The SCA operating principle for Product Life-Cycle Management is:

<u>Long-Term Collaborative Product Planning:</u> Long-term product and sales-channel roadmaps are created collaboratively with simultaneous development of supporting material sourcing, manufacturing, and distribution-planning roadmaps.

Commitment: The organization is committed to defining new product and sales-channel roadmaps for several product generations into the future. These roadmaps are finalized collaboratively across the extended value stream to align on customer expectations, product pricing, product target costing, increased product complexity and demand analysis, and sales-channel implications. This alignment will result in cross-functional agreement relative to manufacturing-system design, material sourcing, supply-chain network requirements, sales and marketing requirements, and overall long-term revenue and total cost implications required to be competitive with this new product.

PRODUCT LIFE-CYCLE MANAGEMENT | SCA SUB-PROCESSES

Relative to SCA and Product Life-Cycle Management, the sub-processes we need to work within are: Product-Selection Planning, Product-Variation Planning, Customer-Service Planning, Material/Service-Sourcing Planning, Inbound Logistics (Sourcing) Planning, Manufacturing Planning, Outbound Logistics (Distribution) Planning, Overall Supply-Chain Network Planning

PRODUCT LIFE-CYCLE MANAGEMENT | SCA METHODS AND TOOLS

The following is a list of methods or tools that are recommended for implementing SCA and the SCA operating principle for Product Life-Cycle Management.

1. **Long-Term Product Roadmap**: Develop a long-term product roadmap, specifically addressing proposed product features and variations, both of which will determine overall complexities and incremental product proliferation introduced into the supply chain. Focus areas are:

   ✸ **Product Plan:** Develop a sustainable product plan for at least three product generations for all markets and sales channels based on extensive market and competitor analysis. Leverage megatrend analysis, target-market analysis, competitor analysis, and functional and user-experience (UX) analysis of customer needs.

   Note: There may be some overlap with work completed in business strategy; however, the work is completed at a deeper level of detail at this stage.

   ✸ **Proven Technologies:** Deploy only proven technologies for the next product generation to avoid excessive startup issues and corresponding waste. Leverage technology-development planning processes, technology scouting and technology-development cooperation scouting, and product-interface studies.

   ✸ **Standardization:** Base customized products on a highly standardized core product with minimum additional components and minimum additional manufacturing. Leverage the development of standardized sub-assemblies and components and component-complexity key-performance indicator analysis.

   ✸ **Postponement**: Design added-value customization to be completed close to the point of customer use in order to create stability and predictability in the upstream supply chain. Leverage supply-chain postponement strategies.

2. **Long-Term Sales-Channel Roadmap**: Connecting to the long-term product roadmap, SCA requires a long-term Sales-Channel Roadmap focusing on market and sales-channel requirements. Thus we can proactively design our supply-chain operations for the long term. We need to ensure that our physical infrastructure and supply-chain processes will meet the needs of future new-product introductions.

   ✸ **Challenge Complexity:** Evaluate and challenge each customized product variation to validate that it is adding value for the customer while contributing to improved market share, increased revenue, and profitability. Each product must be profitable and stand on its own, as cross-subsidization of product portfolios is not a long-term business strategy. Leverage product-variation planning, product-use study, customer value/price analysis, strategic product-variation market-introduction planning, and supply-chain complexity index.

* **Price and Cost Analysis:** Determine product pricing and target cost to ensure profitability. Based on the determined market-price estimate, the total extended value-stream target cost for the product and its components is developed with commitments from product design, material sourcing, and production.

* **Additional Customer Services**: Selected services beyond the product should be based on organizational core competencies in order to strengthen customer relationships and have sustained profitability within the service category. Commit to delivering services with best-in-class quality and a high level of overall supply-chain performance. Leverage customer-service planning, on-site customer teams, responsibility matrix, customer-satisfaction surveys, and joint yearly improvement-planning sessions.

> **Evaluate and challenge each customized product variation to validate that it is adding value for the customer while contributing to improved market share, increased revenue, and profitability.**

* **Sales Channels:** Detail target market and geographical (regions) sales channels by product. Run scenarios and simulation to understand future customer-delivery implications, material sourcing, manufacturing planning, and distribution-infrastructure planning within the current supply-chain network.

3. **Long-Term Supply-Chain Network Design:** Building on the above, proactively design the current-state and ideal-state supply-chain and logistics network, document, and test through simulation and supply-chain network analysis. Complete a network analysis as a blueprint for the physical infrastructure, supply-chain and logistics technology needs, and people-capability requirements that will ultimately support supply-chain operations.

* **Network Design:** Design a high-performing supply-chain network based on realistic product-sales volume scenarios with appropriate manufacturing capabilities being supported by high-performing inbound and outbound logistics processes. Leverage supply-chain and logistics network-design technologies.

* **Make versus Buy:** Drive optimal make-versus-buy decision analysis, where in principle we *make* core technology (differentiating technology that needs to be protected), *make or buy* key technology (technology that is not readily available in the market), and *buy* standard technology (technology with competitive supply base). The goal is to protect our core competencies, focus on priorities, and minimize capital investment while improving flexibility and reducing overall complexity of supply-chain operations.

* **Sourcing and Inbound Logistics:** Proactively design supplier networks, inbound sourcing, supplier management, and inbound logistics processes. Select suppliers based on total cost of ownership (purchase price + cost for quality risks + transportation cost + customs and duties costs + material-inventory cost + potential obsolete-material cost). Understand the implications and cost of complexity in introducing new suppliers with extended lead times and poor performance records.

Note: This is in contrast to selecting suppliers based solely on piece price.

Leverage supplier selection and development programs, inbound network-design simulation, total cost of ownership analysis, and supply-risk analysis.

* **Manufacturing Planning:** Plan for Lean Manufacturing principles to be implemented. Implement a manufacturing system that can produce at the pace of customer demand by remaining flexible and focused on one-piece flow, thus achieving high quality within the shortest possible lead times all while reducing overall effort of people and resources. Understand and ensure that lean manufacturing strategies will connect to outbound logistics processes so true flow of supply-chain operations will be realized.

Note: The absence of this connection between lean manufacturing and distribution will only serve to frustrate the organization as lean efforts in the factory will not produce meaningful results as measured by customer delivery or reduced inventory or operating costs relative to finished goods and outbound logistics.

Leverage manufacturing system design, low-cost automation planning, poka yoke, quick Q feedback loops, 5S, value-stream design, U-shaped lines, TPM, load leveling, kanban, on-board and shop-floor management, A3 problem solving, standardized work, layered process audits, and CIP teams.

✳ **Customer Service and Outbound Logistics:** Proactively design and simulate cost-versus-service tradeoffs relative to planned customer-satisfaction service levels. Complete outbound logistics (distribution) modeling with overall inventory strategies first, with logistics processes designed to support this inventory strategy.

Note: This means we need first to decide what we're going to keep (SKUs), where we're going to keep it (warehouses), how much we're going to keep (supermarket levels), and how we're going to replenish it upon consumption from the planned inventory location (Replenishment Quantities and Transportation).

Leverage outbound logistics-network analysis and simulation, inventory-planning analysis, supply-chain flexibility analysis, supply-chain variation/volume-scenario planning, and customer-service policy planning.

Figure 24 — Product Life-Cycle Management Steps

PRODUCT LIFE-CYCLE MANAGEMENT STEPS

OPERATING PRINCIPLE	Long-Term Collaborative Product Planning
COMMITMENT	Product-Planning Process Sales-Channel Planning Process Supply-Chain Network-Design Process Target-Price & Target-Cost Methodology
SCA TOOLS & METHODS	Long-Term Product Roadmap Long-Term Sales-Channel Roadmap Collaborative New-Product Alignment Long-Term Supply-Chain Network Design

PRODUCT LIFE-CYCLE MANAGEMENT | SUMMARY

Implemented effectively, **<u>Long-Term Collaborative Product Planning</u>** will produce the:

* right voice of customer, customer segment, and sales channels;
* right product differentiation and features for basic market requirements;
* right product variation and customization for special or unique market requirements;
* right realistic sales (demand) volume projections and scenarios;
* right make-or-buy decisions for product and component manufacturing;
* right sourcing (supplier) network and inbound logistics-network footprint;
* right manufacturing system and location concept with the right flexibilities;
* right distribution plan and outbound logistics-network footprint to support the right customer footprint;
* right overall extended value-stream lead time (concept to market); and
* right target cost to support the right market price.

Collaborative Demand and Profit Planning

CHAPTER | 9

SCA Operating Principle

"…if we truly look at it through the lens of our customers, they don't care what goes on inside the business. They want the value, and that's why we're in business."

—MICHAEL EDMUNDS

Sales and Marketing includes the traditional Product, Place, Price, and Promotion focus areas. More specifically, Sales and Marketing entails planning of potential and targeted customer segments, development of distribution and sales channels, planning for multiple customer-delivery techniques (omni-channel), sales promotions, pricing strategies, and product-demand and forecast planning. In total, these processes seek to gain overall advantage in the market by communicating the company's value propositions to distinct market segments, thereby successfully targeting and completing sales to these segments.

Relative to SCA, Sales and Marketing planning processes need to use known and relevant facts about customers to determine realistic short and long term goals for overall sales-volume forecasts by customer, region, and sales channels. This information then needs to connect congruently with supply-chain capabilities and current supply-chain performance. In addition, promotion strategies and new-product launches need to be completed in a collaborative manner with Supply-Chain Operations, where we delve deeply into details relative to customer-delivery agreements and volume expectations. Areas of focus can include delivery locations, lot-size management, delivery frequency, packaging, and leveled-flow strategies, all with the goal of setting clear expectations with our internal operations and our customers. The point here is to avoid making commitments that are completely detached or unrealistic considering current supply-chain operations capabilities.

> **The point here is to avoid making commitments that are completely detached or unrealistic considering current supply-chain operations capabilities.**

Sales and Marketing, in collaboration with core processes, also needs to be responsible and accountable to ensure that all products are profitable in the marketplace by making certain that product features and pricing reflect what customers truly value as well as what complexities (cost) our customers are introducing into our supply chains. It is critical that we get paid for this additional complexity as it is seen as value in the customers' eyes. Therefore the customers should be willing to pay for this value. This articulation of value is a fundamental role of Sales and Marketing.

SALES AND MARKETING | CURRENT-STATE PROBLEMS RELATIVE TO SCA

It is common today, in particular in large organizations, to see a lack of planning and coordination between Product Life-Cycle Management, Sales and Marketing, and Supply-Chain Operations. This results in disconnects at all levels of Supply-Chain Operations and ultimately affects the customer when Supply-Chain Operations have no capability to deliver on promises made. While organizations today are trying to implement Sales and Operations Planning Processes (S&OP), many Sales and Marketing functions continue to act independently of the rest of the business, and their only goal or priority is top-line revenue. Often, this will result in unrealistic and overambitious forecasts that ignore all historical trends, knowledge of the market, and actual supply-chain capabilities (supplier, manufacturing, and distribution capabilities).

In addition, Sales and Marketing and Supply-Chain Operations may be functioning in silos where voice of customer, customer requests for customization of products or services, promises to customers, sales promotions and discounting, and other demand-driven activities are simply thrown over the wall to Supply-Chain Operations with little consideration of organizational capabilities to deliver on the promises made. This will result in the classic situation where Sales and Marketing successfully create demand and believe their job is finished, leaving the rest up to Supply-Chain Operations to deliver the last mile. Then, when the last mile is not successful, the finger pointing and blame game will begin. However, in this classic and all too common example, nobody should be blamed as everybody is simply managing and reacting to current business strategies, current performance targets and KPIs, and current levels of collaboration (or lack of collaboration). In other words, everybody is doing exactly what the business and management system is asking them to do. In the end though, all it creates is chaos and instability relative to supply-chain performance and customer satisfaction.

An example of misguided commitments is the case where management principles state "we will never say no to a customer" without any understanding of actual supply-chain performance capabilities or the complexities and waste that will be introduced by blindly fulfilling any customer request. In this case, you may never say *no* to a customer, but you will often not deliver on promises made.

Performance targets and KPIs in Sales and Marketing often focus on top-line sales without regard for the bottom-line profitability of the transaction. Once again, nobody is to blame for this situation as the system is designed with this purpose in mind. In many cases, the organization gets what the performance targets reward, which may be a high level of sales volume that Supply-Chain Operations struggles to meet, all at prices that do not deliver value (profit) to the organization or shareholders.

These situations need to change for Advanced Supply-Chain Performance to be realized.

Collaboratively across all four core business processes, we need to begin asking ourselves:

1. Is this demand true customer demand (based on customer request and plausibility checks at that time), and will the sale actually provide bottom-line profit for the organization?
2. Relative to the state of our Supply-Chain Operations capability, is it

realistic in any way to assume that we can actually meet the promises made to the customer?

3. If our customer is asking for additional complexities in products and services, how will we ensure we are compensated for this additional value?

4. What is creating the fundamental disconnect inside our organization that allows us to make promises to customers that we clearly will never be able to deliver upon in a profitable fashion?

Another important element relative to Sales and Marketing and SCA surrounds *Voice of Customer (VOC)*. When we think of VOC, we typically think of product features, product benefits, and customer-driven innovation. What's missing here is VOC relative to supply-chain dynamics. We fail to understand how our customers consume our products, how they determine order quantities, lead-time requirements, delivery locations, replenishment strategies, and logistics processes that may drive instability in our own supply-chain operations. These constitute very important input when one of our overall SCA goals is to implement flow and stability across the extended value stream. We want our customers' consumption of our product to act as the pace setter for our supply-chain operations, so we need to temper our enthusiasm for creating false demand. In other words, let's not be our own worst enemy.

An example of this concept is when we create false demand through promotions and discounting where we at times force (too good to pass up) customers to buy product they don't need at that particular time. This false demand creates significant noise in their supply chain (transportation, storage, inventory control), and it produces customer-demand information in our supply chain that is completely detached from reality. In many cases, we may actually replenish our own supply chain based on this false customer demand and then be surprised when the customer has not ordered more products for months. This is a perpetual negative self-fulfilling prophecy, as the more you do it the more you will have to do it in order to meet monthly revenue goals. Certainly these transactions may produce revenue, but they will not be producing significant profit. In most cases they will be producing losses when viewed from a total-cost point of view across the extended value stream.

Another point relative to Sales and Marketing is the reality of most customer-service failures. Most often a service failure is not attributed to product features or benefits (a big part of typical VOC), but rather the fact that we did not deliver the right product to the right place at the right time or in the right quantity. These failure modes are service failures that VOC processes within Sales and Marketing may capture, but it may not always communicate details effectively to supply-chain operations in a timely manner. In these cases, we miss the opportunity to understand our customers' true concerns, and we also may fail to learn about upcoming customer changes to product requirements or ordering patterns. Sales and Marketing efforts need to bring this intelligence back from customer operations in order for us to solve problems proactively and get ahead of customer expectations or upcoming changes in customer requirements.

> **We want our customers' consumption of our product to act as the pace setter for our supply-chain operations, so we need to temper our enthusiasm for creating false demand.**

At this point you may think that as authors we are negative on Sales and Marketing. Nothing could be farther from the truth. Sales and Marketing is a critical core process of any business, and there are extremely talented Sales and Marketing executives within organizations we work with. However, what we do lack, and what SCA is focused on, is the connection between Sales and Marketing and the other three core processes, in particular Supply-Chain Operations.

It is this connection that SCA strives to create and sustain in order to deliver stability of product flow and profitability across the extended value stream.

SALES AND MARKETING | IDEAL STATE RELATIVE TO SCA

Sales and Marketing is highly collaborative across the extended value stream and gathers and delivers timely and factual customer intelligence in all aspects of Voice of Customer (VOC). This VOC includes product-information requirements but also supply-chain operations requirements and a high level of knowledge relative to anticipated customer-quantity needs and how products are consumed and replenished within the customer environment. Sales and Marketing collaborates with Supply-Chain Operations to identify what customer commitments should be entered into relative to current supply-chain capabilities. Therefore Sales and Marketing and Supply-Chain Operations collectively determine what business-improvement priorities should be set when current supply-chain capabilities are not acceptable. Sales and Marketing ensures that the organization is making realistic promises to customers and that we are paid properly for these commitments when additional complexity is introduced into our organization. In doing so, when the customer promise is met, it will deliver value to the customer and also value to the organization in the form of bottom-line profit generation by product.

SCA OPERATING PRINCIPLE
SALES AND MARKETING

The SCA operating principle for Sales and Marketing is:

Collaborative Demand and Profit Planning: Highly collaborative customer demand, production, and material planning, with a goal of stable and profitable sales growth.

Commitment: The organization is committed to planning all demand implications across the extended value stream. Supply-chain activities are integrated with Sales and Marketing activities, which are based on real customer demand acting as the pace setter across the end-to-end supply-chain network. Customer commitments are made with a deep understanding of how our customers consume our products, recognizing realistic supply-chain capabilities; and the organization is committed to eliminating any activities that result in false demand signals or the production (procurement) of products (material) that are not required by the customer. All products are expected to generate contribution to profit; we collaboratively measure ourselves by profitable sales results; and all products that cannot generate appropriate profit are retired from the product portfolio.

SALES AND MARKETING | SCA SUB-PROCESSES

Relative to SCA and Sales and Marketing, the sub-processes we need to work within are: Voice-of-Customer Processes, Sales-Channel Planning, Sales-Promotion Planning, Customer-Delivery Agreement Planning, Sales-Forecast and Demand Planning, and Sales and Operations Planning.

SALES AND MARKETING | SCA METHODS AND TOOLS

The following is a list of methods or tools that are recommended for implementing SCA and the SCA operating principle for Sales and Marketing.

1. **Voice of Customer (VOC):** VOC processes need to evolve beyond product features and move into customer experience relative to the customer's connection to our supply-chain operations. We need to gather customer feedback for improvement in relation to our overall supply-chain capabilities. This is the essence of SCA, where we use supply-chain performance as a feedback mechanism to set internal business-improvement priorities.

   ❋ **Customer-Connected Supply Chains:** We require deep dialogue with our customers about how our supply-chain operations connect to their operations. This dialogue will produce the information we require not only to understand current performance but also to gather early notification of customer changes. This will allow us to attempt to create level flow by connecting our supply-chain operations directly to our customers' actual consumption patterns. It is critical that we understand our customers' supply-chain operations in order for us to forecast more accurate demand quantities and hence our own supply-chain operations requirements. To accomplish this, leverage collaborative customer-supplier joint value-stream mapping exercises.

   ❋ **Customer Agreements:** We need to work closely with our customers to align on product-delivery agreements, supply-chain risk sharing (e.g., exchange-rate risk, transportation interruptions), stability in customer forecast and fixed-order horizons that result in commitments, shared or planned inventory positions in the extended value stream, customer-delivery locations, supplier shipping locations, lot size, packaging, frequency-of-delivery determination, ownership of transportation/logistics/inventory cost for normal operation and emergency expediting (detailing the different reasons for emergencies), and customer interfacing for demand planning and notification of probable changes in demand patterns.

   We must recognize that this is a level of rigor that customers may not be comfortable with, so the value of these conversations needs to be articulated. This value needs to be driven by waste identification, complexity avoidance, and ultimately lower costs and lower prices for all supply-chain partners. It is imperative that we show the value of this work by setting goals for measured business results for all stake holders. To accomplish this, leverage formal customer meetings to create transparency and dialogue relative to supply-chain operation challenges and possible collaborative solutions.

Note: We don't want to sound naïve with this work, and we recognize that not all customer relationships will be at this level of collaboration. However, these are the activities and next frontier for significant waste reduction and advanced supply-chain performance.

* **Customer Complexity Requests:** VOC processes need to drive a rigorous understanding of supply chain-related complexities requested by our customers. These can include packaging requests, labeling requirements, lot-size requests, delivery parameters, or other logistics requirements that add complexity to our operations. The goal is to understand the perceived value to the customer if the request introduces new complexity (cost) into our operations. Once the complexity and value are understood, we will be better prepared to support internally and to articulate to the customer why there should be compensation for this additional value.

  We always want to satisfy customer requests. In doing so, we show fundamental respect for our customers. In this same spirit, our customers should expect us to show ourselves an equal amount of internal respect. This means we need to have clear and agreed-upon rules of engagement with our customers and we should be able to open up pricing dialogue when customers ask for increased services or complexity to be introduced into our supply chains.

2. **Extended Value-Stream Demand Planning:** Customer and demand-planning activities require an extended value-stream perspective. This means formal management processes where we collaboratively discuss plan vs. actual relative to:

* Are planned new products on time, and what is the most recent expectation for demand volumes during ramp-up, at running rate, with seasonality, before and after product model changes, across all channels?

* What customer support and service is needed during new-product launches?
* What sales promotions are in the pipeline, and what is the expected impact on sales volumes by product?
* What planning and action are required in outbound distribution, manufacturing, and inbound supply-chain activities for better alignment with the customer?

These questions are the essence of extended value-stream demand planning, where we continuously use new and improved market intelligence to compare supply-chain capabilities and required activities to achieve the goal.

Note: Many organizations have sales and operations-planning (S&OP) processes in place; this extended value-stream demand planning is a logical extension of this process.

* **Customer-Demand Planning:** It's important to ensure that customer contracts are clear regarding deliverables such as product features, product performance, beyond-the-product services, total-contract sales volume, ramp-up volumes, anticipated yearly volumes, seasonal (periodic) low and high volumes, and detailed delivery requirements, with sales pricing developed relative to these agreements. As discussed above, we need to eliminate the complexity created by allowing excessive, non-market-driven customer- demand schedule changes. These include self-created or customer-created forms of instability that keep us from achieving improvement in leveling our demand planning.

  Evaluate and act upon customer consumption and inventory data (as per supply delivery agreements), market data of customer sales to their end customer, customer market-share development, industry-inventory development, and available economic development data to understand better the flow of product to your customer. In case of major deviations from your plan, formally discuss these results with the customer, seek understanding, gather revised customer-demand data, and act upon this information to avoid excessive inventories. Ensure that customer contracts have the necessary clarity on dynamics that affect supply-chain performance. Analyze customer sales fluctuation (sales-pipeline fill volume, model changes, sales ramp-up, seasonal and promotional impacts);

discuss the required flexibility/cost with the customer and align supply-chain system inventory accordingly. Do not accept excessive, non-market-driven, customer-demand schedule changes, and where required conduct customer workshops to identify root causes and improvements to stabilize demand schedules.

* **Base-Volume Determination:** In an ideal world, customer-demand volumes would be completely stable and supply-chain operations would be perfectly matched to fulfill this stable level of demand. Unfortunately, demand is not perfectly stable, so we are left with unstable and erratic activities within supply-chain operations in order to predict, react to, and fulfill unleveled customer-demand patterns. However, all organizations have some level of stable demand volume. There is some stable volume expectation, by product, that the organization can rely on. Once we have this base volume we can plan stable supply-chain operations to produce this base level of predictable demand consistently. Once established, volumes above this base volume can be dealt with as incremental to the base supply-chain operations. In other words, we have an extremely stable end-to-end supply-chain operation plan on a stable base volume, and we will deal with additional volumes on a case-by-case basis through our extended value-stream demand-planning process.

  Managing demand fluctuations from the base case upwards changes the conversation significantly as it allows more focused and challenging dialogue on expected new volumes, and it allows us to plan supplier, manufacturing, and distribution activities on incremental demand as opposed to all demand. To accomplish this goal, we need to leverage Sales and Marketing to produce customer, product, and market intelligence that results in our understanding and calculation of stable base-volume expectations by product and sales channel.

* **Sales-Promotion Management:** Sales promotions are creative approaches to stimulating demand. For purposes of SCA we will assume they are required for some industries, although it is easy from a supply-chain (and profit) perspective to argue that sales promotions may be the disease as opposed to the cure. What is critical, though, is that sales promotions are connected to supply-chain operations and to profit generation.

There is nothing more damaging than a sales promotion being supported by empty shelves, or the opposite where overflowing shelves (inventory) are in fact the cause for the sales promotion.

Formally plan sales promotion well in advance with realistic sales-volume forecasts, and be highly participative with supply-chain operations to mini-

> **Once we have this base volume we can plan stable supply-chain operations to produce this base level of predictable demand consistently.**

mize potential supply-chain disruption and maximize value to the customer at the lowest possible total cost to the business. We need to be smart and strategic about promotional activity, where promotions are used to gain new market share or support other strategic initiatives. Most importantly, sales promotions require a viable path to contributing to profit. Sales promotions used to generate cash, meet month-end revenue targets, or dump excess inventories are not strategic. These types of sales promotions are an indication of serious problems within the extended value stream of the organization.

3. **Product Profitability:** Generating profit is the responsibility of the entire business. It's not reasonable to believe that *if all functions of the business focus on their own part, profit will result*. Hidden profit is accomplished through extended value-stream management with highly participative and collaborative leadership. To this end, Sales and Marketing activities need to drive profitable revenue growth. Top line and bottom line.

We need to leverage visibility and management around profit rationalization at all customers, products (SKUs – part numbers), sales channels, and geographical regions. Select sales opportunities with agreed-upon profit targets, and evaluate target pricing and total cost of doing business with each customer, product, and sales channel. These profit-planning activities will require collaboration across the extended value stream, and alignment and agreement should lead to successful supply-chain operation preparation to support sales activities successfully.

Last, feedback from post-sales activity gathered from supply-chain operations should be used to validate assumptions and actual results from the sales and marketing activities.

Figure 25 — *Sales & Marketing Steps*

SALES & MARKETING STEPS

OPERATING PRINCIPLE	*Collaborative Demand and Profit Planning*
COMMITMENT	Required Visibility Across Extended Value Stream Collaborative Sales Promotions Visible and Realistic Customer Commitments Profit Contribution by each Product
SCA TOOLS & METHODS	Voice-of-Customer Methodology Extended Value-Stream Demand Planning Collaborative Sales-Promotion Planning Product-Profitability Analysis

SALES AND MARKETING | SUMMARY

Implemented effectively, **<u>Collaborative Demand and Profit Planning</u>** will produce the:

* right process to make collaborative and effective customer commitments;
* right promotions and sales activities relative to supply-chain capabilities;
* right price by customer and sales channels based on the right target costing to determine product needs and demand-consumption patterns;
* right processes to monitor continually voice-of-customer on quality and delivery;
* right delivery and supply agreements with suppliers and customers recognizing supply-chain capabilities;
* right data to make the right supplier-sourcing and manufacturing decisions based on expected customer consumption of our products; and
* right profit at each product or part number (SKU), customer, sales channel, and region level.

Reliable Delivery + Speed and Visible Flow

CHAPTER | 10

SCA Operating Principle

"…supply-chain leaders have to be internal salespeople. They have to talk intelligently in a language everyone can understand."

—RICK D. BLASGEN

Supply-Chain Operations is the core process designed to fulfill customer orders. It is the value stream (network) created when we connect the physical flow processes of: raw-material sourcing, inbound logistics, manufacturing, and outbound customer-order fulfillment. In today's world of e-commerce, it is also important to add reverse logistics to this definition. In addition, supply-chain activities include the processes that enable information flow that facilitates physical material flow within inbound and outbound logistics processes. These include supply, demand and production planning, supplier management, purchasing, inbound logistics, manufacturing, outbound logistics (order fulfillment), customer-service (order) functions, and reverse logistics.

The core purpose of Supply-Chain Operations is to facilitate the flow of product and information from supplier through manufacturing and distribution to the ultimate customer. Consequently, supply-chain operations is the final connection point to the customer. It is also the final reservoir or landing spot of outcomes from decisions made in other core processes of the business. Ultimately, intended and unintended consequences from all business decisions and the resulting planned and unplanned complexity will manifest themselves in the supply chain.

SUPPLY-CHAIN OPERATIONS | CURRENT-STATE PROBLEMS RELATIVE TO SCA

Understanding supply-chain operation challenges relative to SCA requires a perspective from two vantage points. One is supply-chain disconnects across all core processes (extended value stream), and the second is the series of disconnects with supply-chain operations itself.

At an extended value-stream level, the fundamental challenge is that supply-chain operations are not integrated or connected with other core processes. In many respects this is the sole reason SCA is required. The result is that supply-chain operations are highly reactive; they are simply reacting to decisions made upstream in the business. A small set of examples of these upstream decisions are: new-product introductions with increased manufacturing complexities, supplier-selection decisions (that result in longer lead times), sales promotions, and sales-channel decisions resulting in more complex logistics processes. The list of examples is endless because all business decisions will eventually have implications in the supply chain.

The second challenge that exists is that supply-chain operations are prone to disconnects within the core process itself. In the last decade, many organizations have attempted to improve flow across the *end-to-end supply chain*. This end-to-end supply chain is defined as the network created when we begin at our customer and work our way upstream through manufacturing and continue upstream to the tier-one supplier. If we are more aggressive, we can work farther upstream into tier-two and tier-three suppliers.

> The problem is that implementing lean manufacturing will not produce significant business results unless the flow and velocity are connected to the supply-base capabilities upstream and the customer-consumption takt (demand rhythm) downstream.

This end-to-end work has the objective of implementing flow and velocity across the entire supply chain. Most of our work started within the manufacturing process in order to implement lean manufacturing principles. However, the problem is that implementing lean manufacturing will not produce significant business results unless the flow and velocity are connected to the supply-base capabilities upstream and the customer-consumption takt (demand rhythm) downstream. This lack of connection means that while we are able to build product in smaller batches and higher manufacturing frequencies, we don't actually create end-to-end flow or eliminate waste in inbound and outbound supply-chain activities.

Note: We are very strong advocates of lean manufacturing and are very hopeful SCA will allow organizations to benefit from their lean work and investment.

A third challenge that exists today, and one that is very relevant to SCA, is the fact that most businesses do not recognize the extreme value of supply-chain operations feedback. We strategically design and sell products and services, we work extremely hard to fulfill customer orders, and then we simply move on to the next thing. We rarely take time to examine and reflect upon the actual results of past decisions or projects. The result of this situation is a supply chain that is burdened with excessive inventories, extended lead times, unstable processes, and unreliable performance due to the fact that we are always moving on to the next emergency and not cleaning up our past initiatives. In addition and already discussed at length, this situation also means we are not leveraging opportunities to identify priorities for business-improvement opportunities that will result in extracting hidden profit.

The last challenge we will call out is visibility. Far too many organizations are simply operating without any visibility of what is actually going on in the business. The result is that all core processes and sub-processes only see what is right in front of them, and decisions are made with this myopic single-process view of the operation. Organizations have not taken the time to understand what we need to see, how we will make it visible, or what we will do with the information we gather once it is visible. Yet in the absence of this visibility, we simply continue to make decisions based on *what's best for me* as opposed to what is best to maximize customer value at the lowest possible total cost to the business.

SUPPLY-CHAIN OPERATIONS | IDEAL STATE RELATIVE TO SCA

Supply-Chain Operations are planned, visible, stable, reliable, and highly collaborative, and they provide an operational-feedback loop. Supply-chain initiatives relentlessly focus on end-to-end flow, speed, and lead-time reduction by identifying and eliminating all non-value complexities and waste. This is accomplished through rigorous process discipline, inventory reduction, and first-time quality of processes. The supply chain flows to the pace of customer demand, where all supply-chain activities are triggered by the pull of the pace-setting process. The goal of supply-chain operations is to deliver the highest value to the customer at the lowest possible total cost.

SCA OPERATING PRINCIPLE
SUPPLY-CHAIN OPERATIONS

The SCA operating principle for Supply-Chain Operations is:

Reliable Delivery + Speed and Visible Flow: Highly reliable delivery and capable speed with end-to-end supply-chain visibility focused on implementing and controlling leveled flow and velocity across an extremely stable and reliable logistics network.

Commitment: The organization is committed to having a core competency in supply-chain operations. We understand our supply-chain capabilities and make commitments knowing we will be dependable and reliable in meeting promises made. We operate with highly visible material and information flow across the end-to-end supply chain and are in relentless pursuit of lead-time reduction and leveled flow. Real customer consumption acts as the only pace-setting process for the entire network, and replenishment processes are triggered by this pace (customer takt). Hour-to-hour supply-chain activities are monitored and controlled, where supplier, manufacturing, and customer-delivery performance is captured and used to identify problems and prioritize business-improvement activities. Logistics network operations are designed to flow inbound materials and outbound finished products based on balancing speed and total operational cost across the network. Product-inventory levels are continuously monitored, scrutinized, and corrected to ensure only profitable products (material) remain in the supply chain. Feedback from inventory corrections is provided to the SCA team for review of past assumptions made, lessons learned, and business-improvement opportunities identified.

SUPPLY-CHAIN OPERATIONS | SCA SUB-PROCESSES

Relative to SCA and Supply-Chain Operations, the sub-processes we need to work within are Material Planning and Procurement, Inbound Logistics, Production Planning, Manufacturing and Production Control, Customer-Order Management, Outbound Logistics, and Reverse Logistics.

SUPPLY-CHAIN OPERATIONS | SCA METHODS AND TOOLS

The following is a list of methods or tools that are recommended for implementing SCA and the SCA operating principle for Supply-Chain Operations.

1. **Visibility Management:** Visibility is a management method in and of itself. This needs to be a CEO-led campaign to identify what needs to be visible, make it visible, and have processes and structures in place to act upon the information gained from the visibility. Could we imagine an airport that did not have a control tower, where airport employees did not know what they needed to see or how to act once a situation was made visible? Our businesses are no different.

   Relative to supply-chain operations, visibility needs to take an extended value-stream and end-to-end supply-chain view where we create visibility based on the past, present, and future.

   * **Past:** What visibility do we need relative to yesterday so we can create an SCA feedback loop and challenge past decisions, prioritize business-improvement initiatives, and make better decisions going forward as a group of informed and highly participative leaders?

❋ **Present:** What do we need to see today (hour by hour) and in real time to create the transparency and visibility needed to plan versus actual conditions and process problems relative to physical flow of material and information in the supply chain?

❋ **Future:** What visibility do we need across the extended value stream relative to our belief of what will happen in the future so we can pro-actively initiate supply chain-centric decision making to avoid unintended consequences and unplanned complexity being introduced into the supply chain?

> This control tower will be monitoring the plan relative to: what is heading through distribution to our customers, what is heading in and out of the manufacturing facilities, and what is moving within the inbound supply-chain and supplier network. This coordinated control process is continuously looking at inventories and identifying inventory that is not producing profit for the organization.

A plan can be created from an extended value-stream map, where we focus specifically on what we need from a visibility point of view. From there, we need to leverage current technologies and embrace new technologies that focus on visibility of material and product flow. Last, we need to leverage the *control tower* concept. Similar to the airport control tower, all organizations need a coordinated control center that is watching and acting upon end-to-end supply-chain activities in real time. This control tower will be monitoring the plan relative to: what is heading through distribution to our customers, what is heading in and out of the manufacturing facilities, and what is moving within the inbound supply-chain and supplier network. This coordinated control process is continuously looking at inventories and identifying inventory that is not producing profit for the organization.

Note: Most organizations will need to establish this control tower concept. Please consider it a basic cost of doing business, and rest assured it will produce significant return on investment as measured by captured revenue, reduced operating costs, and working-capital improvements.

2. **End-to-End Supply-Chain Management:** Think of this as SCA for supply chain only. It is critical that we connect the end-to-end supply chain, even

in the absence of full extended value-stream connections. This means we need to understand customer consumption and connect distribution with both manufacturing and the inbound supply chain to create true flow and velocity. The ultimate goal is a mentality and operation that support *if the customer buys one . . . then we replenish one just in time.*

Leverage an end-to-end supply-chain stream value map with a focus specifically on flow and connection of adjacent processes, beginning at the customer and working upstream into the supply chain. Focus on one SKU to start, and determine the true demand patterns for this SKU. Then map the upstream supply chain relative to inventory and lead time, and compare this to actual customer demand and customer lead-time expectations. This will highlight the disconnections between supply-chain processes with respect to inventory levels, batch sizes, order quantities, transportation processes, warehouse processes, supplier performance, manufacturing performance, and overall lead times required to meet customer demand with minimal effort and just in time.

3. **Flow and Speed:** Flow and speed are an actual management method and are part of any operational excellence initiative. Flow and speed (velocity) are tactical techniques that result in lead-time reduction across the end-to-end supply chain. The theory is that the faster material and product flow through the supply chain, the less waste that exists in the supply chain. This is intuitive as lead time is only made up of two things, value and waste. Product is either flowing towards the customer (value) or it is not (waste).

Consider this. If we buy a raw component from our supplier, will it flow from the supplier to our manufacturing facility and then continue to flow to the customer as a finished good, all without ever stopping? If the answer is no, then what are the reasons it stops? This list of reasons will become our problem-solving work relative to flow and speed.

Leverage *Plan for Every Part (PFEP)* to enable pull replenishment based on customer consumption. Create speed (velocity) by optimizing lot sizes, delivery frequencies, inventory levels, leveling, and supporting logistics processes across the end-to-end supply chain. Ensure that we connect and attempt to level the critical logistics processes of: raw-material ordering, inbound transportation, inbound warehousing, manufacturing, outbound transportation, outbound warehousing, and customer-order management.

4. **Quality at the Source:** Advanced supply-chain performance is also reliable and predictable supply-chain performance. We will not succeed in connecting the extended value stream if functions and adjacent processes do not trust each other. It is not uncommon for a large portion of system inventory to be in the system for no other reason than that the system itself is not trusted. A main reason supply-chain operations are not reliable is because processes are not disciplined, coordinated, connected, visible, capable, or dependable. Yes, there is a lot here, but much of this can be overcome with a focus on quality at the source (first-time quality). As leaders, we should expect and support the development of robust supply-chain processes that *get it right the first time* and only send good product and good information downstream towards the customer.

Identify and leverage the standardization of critical-to-quality value-added processes. Eliminate or automate all non-critical transactional processes by leveraging technologies and best practices already available to the organization. Error proof critical processes through visual management, standard work, and first-time quality toll gates.

This focus on process discipline will need to be extended downstream to customers, upstream to suppliers, and across logistics processes where third-party logistics providers are stake holders in our supply chain. Processes need to be designed and managed with full expectations of rigor and first-time quality. When processes fail, responsibility and accountability are required in order to understand root causes, introduce immediate containment strategies, and execute solutions for long-term countermeasures.

The goal of Quality at the Source is to ensure critical processes are visible, stable, and predictable so that collectively we will trust the system and eliminate all buffers (waste) that exist as protection for perceived unreliability.

5. **Complexity Management:** Complexity management is a major theme of SCA. We have addressed this already relative to product development and sales and marketing complexities across the extended value stream. However, complexity management needs to have focus within the end-to-end supply chain specifically. The whole organization should be leveraging supply-chain

operations to identify and bring transparency to complexity proliferation relative to: customers, finished goods, logistics providers, warehouses, transportation systems, manufacturing facilities, inventory levels, packaging requirements, raw materials, and suppliers.

It needs to be stated clearly and supported with SCA operating principles that the organization can no longer sustain the introduction of complexities that neither add value to the customer nor provide profit to the organization.

Leverage the SCA complexity index and educate the organization on complexity elimination. The first goal is to *do no more harm* by not inserting new unplanned complexity, and from there we need to identify and reverse wasteful complexity that has previously been introduced. This can be accomplished by leveraging current best practices within the organization, best use of current technologies, suppliers, and materials, all with the goal of standardization of processes across the supply chain.

Note: SCA and supply chain-centric decision making will be the largest driver of fighting this complexity.

6. **Performance Management:** Performance is implied in SCA. However, it is critical that performance management should be a specific management method. This method will dovetail with our SCA management system, visibility, and reliability initiatives. This includes our process to set and align around measurable extended value-stream goals with clear responsibility and accountability to achieve the targeted results. To that end, supply-chain operations needs to facilitate the communication of our actual results to the organization. In other words, supply-chain operations needs to have visibility, relevant metrics, and the platform to declare, *This was our plan across the extended value stream, this is what we did, and this is the result. And this is what we can learn from it!*

Figure 26 — *Supply-Chain Operations Steps*

SUPPLY-CHAIN OPERATIONS STEPS

OPERATING PRINCIPLE	*Reliable Delivery + Speed and Visible Flow*
COMMITMENT	Supply-Chain Core Competency Highly Visible Material and Information Flow Logistics Network Design for Velocity Dependable and Reliable Process Performance
SCA TOOLS & METHODS	Visibility Management End-to-End Supply-Chain Management Flow + Speed and Quality at the Source Complexity and Performance Management

SUPPLY-CHAIN OPERATIONS | SUMMARY

Implemented effectively, **Reliable Delivery + Speed and Visible Flow** will produce the:

* right logistics network to deliver reliably the right products from the right sources at the right time with the right quality in the right quantity and right place;
* right supplier and manufacturing performance (safety, delivery, quality, cost);
* right replenishment processes triggered by the right customer demand;
* right inventory levels and right logistics cost to produce the right profitability; and
* right visibility and right supply-chain feedback to identify the right business-improvement activities.

SCA Key Performance Indicators

CHAPTER | 11

"…alignment is absolutely critical. If top level goals and strategies are not well communicated by senior leaders, that makes tradeoff decisions much more difficult and creates misalignment and conflict within the organization."

—HEATHER SHEEHAN

Performance measurements, target setting, and Key Performance Indicators (KPIs) are a staple in any business. Depending on the size of the organization, there may be hundreds if not thousands of formal and informal KPIs in place. *You get what you measure* is supposed to be a positive argument for having metrics on everything, building on the well known *Hawthorne Effect* of improvement through attention giving. However, it begs the question, *What if you are measuring the wrong things?* You will be in tough shape if you do in fact get what you measure.

As mentioned in the first few chapters, as authors we have been witness to many underwhelming attempts at Total Quality Management, Six Sigma, and Lean implementations. While there are many contributing causes for this underperformance, there is no question that single-process focused performance management and KPIs are at the top of the list of culprits. Many organizations would actually be better off with no KPIs at all, supporting the Hippocratic Oath of *Do no harm*.

It has been implied in multiple parts of the book so far, but let's summarize very real and very typical examples of KPIs driving destructive and waste-generating activities within the organization.

* Product Development achieves its new-product launch goals regarding features and timing, all at the expense of increased technology risk, missed target cost, and increased non-value-added complexity across the entire supply chain.
* Sales and Marketing achieve their revenue goals, while the organization loses money on each unit sold during the campaign.
* Procurement achieves its bill-of-material unit-cost down goals, all at the expense of increased supplier lead time, reduced supplier performance, and overall increase to total logistics cost across the end-to-end supply chain.
* Logistics achieves its transportation and warehousing efficiency goals, all at the expense of moving and storing inventory that is not required by the customer.
* Manufacturing reaches its productivity targets by reducing change-overs and decreasing lot sizes, all while building product (inventory) that has absolutely no immediate customer demand in the marketplace.

This list doesn't paint a very attractive picture, which makes us ask, *Why is this happening*? The answer to this question may be different depending on the organization, but we are certain two causes will be evident in every case.

* Targets and KPIs are single-process focused and do not represent the health of the business across the extended value stream or the end-to-end supply chain.
* The management and target-review system within the organization does not drive dialogue and investigation relative to how the KPI is being achieved.

For example, take the situation where a factory meets its goal for total number of products built, and this is sent to the corporate office for review, whereupon all looks fine and everybody is happy and rewarded for the great result. In this case, there is no supporting information or process KPI talking to the approach or methods used to achieve the goal.

Let's build upon this example, and picture a scenario where the plant manager sends a note with the KPI that says, *This KPI was achieved by building a large quantity of product A, not because we have demand for product A, but because that's what we had raw materials to build. The product has now been transported in truck-load quantities to the finished-goods warehouse, which will help them achieve their cost per case storage goals!*

We suspect a note like this or a process KPI (e.g., production-schedule achievement by product type) would and should create some dialogue in the organization. This is the purpose of SCA. While this example may not seem pleasant, this is precisely the type of operational realities that exist and that are draining us of hidden profit.

This will be very tough for some of us to digest; however, building upon this example, from a profit point of view the organization would be better off with a note from the plant manager that says, *I did not achieve my KPI today because we did not build anything. I did not have the raw materials needed to build what is currently being demanded. We have launched formal problem solving in close collaboration with inbound supply chain to identify and fix the root causes of the raw-material shortages . . . more to follow.*

> The management and target-review system within the organization must drive dialogue and investigation relative to how the KPI is being achieved.

The good news is, if we implement the SCA Management System and Supply Chain-Centric Decision Making as previously outlined, we will be certain to begin this level of dialogue.

SCA KEY PERFORMANCE INDICATORS

It's easy to point out all the problems and challenges with KPIs. Consequently, it's very important to us as authors that we produce some ideas on how to meet these challenges.

For SCA purposes, we will identify specific target areas for key performance indicators (KPIs). We recognize some of these may exist today or may be new to the current list of KPIs used for performance management. That being the case, as SCA work progresses, we will need to review all KPIs and their relationship and value to extended value-stream thinking.

We will list SCA-recommended key performance indicators in two categories. The first are *leading* or *process indicators (PI),* and the second are *lagging* or *result indicators (RI).* The theory is that if we improve the process indicators (PI) we will see improvement in the important result indicators (RI). This is going back to high school algebra where we learned that Y is a function of X. Consider process indicators to be the Xs and result indicators to be the Ys.

Note: We understand that from an extended value-stream perspective many of these KPIs will be new and difficult for the organization to gather data and create the dashboard for. The work required to create SCA-KPIs will be valuable in itself relative to making business-improvement opportunities visible. We ask that you go through the KPIs with a mind open to the value of attempting to establish these KPIs within the organization, where value is defined as creating visibility and transparency for hidden profit that currently exists within the business.

We have intentionally tried to keep this list of KPIs to a critical few. We don't want KPIs to be a strategy looking for a problem, and we don't want SCA to turn into a data-gathering exercise. It is important to understand that the KPI is not the goal, but rather the goal is the result achieved with the help of the KPI to guide our attention and focus.

SCA AND KPIs

In a perfect SCA world, we would have a dashboard that would simply tell us how we are doing across the extended value stream relative to the Ten Rights. That is, at the end of each day we would answer the question, How did we do in getting 1) the right products, 2) to the right customers, 3) in the right quantities, 4) in the right quality, 5) at the right times, 6) from the right sources, 7) at the right prices, 8) at the right total cost, 9) with the right services, 10) all within the right amount of required complexity (effort) across the extended value stream?

While this is ideal, we recognize it will be challenging for an organization with any scale. However, this needs to be the starting point for dialogue within leadership. We suggest this as a very valuable workshop and dialogue for the organization, as the attempt to measure the Ten Rights across the extended value stream will be similar to learning a new language. While it will be challenging at first, this is one of the beginning conversations of discovering hidden profit.

In the end though, our goal is to establish a dashboard that can be used by the entire organization to validate and develop confidence that SCA efforts are delivering real and significant business results.

SCA KEY PERFORMANCE INDICATORS (PI + RI = KPI):

Note: For all of these KPIs, assume they are being measured to a target where the SCA management system is driving dialogue around the KPI relative to Plan vs. Actual condition.

For the below, we will distinguish between Process Indicators (PI) and Result Indicators (RI).

SCA Process Indicators (PI):

* *Extended Value-Stream Lead Time:* From product concept to first delivery to customer.
* *End-to-End Supply-Chain Lead Time:* Dock-to-dock time from supplier to customer. Look at supplier inbound lead time + manufacturing lead time + outbound distribution lead time.
* *Product Complexity Index:* The complexity index relative to supply-chain drivers, e.g., number of suppliers, number of components, number of finished goods, all compared to revenue from past years.
* *Supply-Chain Complexity Index:* Volume of warehouses (total sq. feet) and number of warehouses, material-handling transactions, transportation partners, 3PLs, and transportation lead times, all compared to revenue from previous years.
* *Supplier Performance:* Safety, quality, delivery, responsiveness, lead time, interruptions, and total cost.
* *Inbound Logistics Performance:* Safety, quality, delivery, responsiveness, lead time, interruptions, and total cost.
* *Manufacturing Performance:* Safety, quality, delivery, responsiveness, lead time, interruptions, and total cost.
* *Outbound Logistics (Distribution) Performance:* Safety, quality, delivery, responsiveness, lead time, interruptions, and total cost.

* ***Inventory Positions (Levels):*** Inventory in supply-chain operations (analysis by SKU on inventory levels, velocity, and turns of every SKU by SKU). Identify and eliminate all dead stock and redesign levels and replenishment for slow-moving inventory.
* ***Retired SKUs vs. New-SKU Introduction:*** Attempt to have an equal number or more SKUs retired for all SKUs introduced.
* ***End-to-End Supply-Chain Cost:*** Total network cost incurred by supply-chain operations.

SCA Result Indicators (RI):

* ***Total Sales Revenue:*** Target achievement versus strategic plan relative to products, markets, regions, channels, and customers.
* ***Total Product Cost:*** Target achievement versus strategic plan relative to base products and product variances across the extended value stream.
* ***Total Inventory:*** (Raw Material + Work-in-Progress + Finished Goods) versus strategic plan relative to products, markets, regions, channels, and customers.
* ***Cash-to-Cash Cycle Time:*** Defined by Accounts Receivable (days) + (plus) Total Inventory (days)–(minus) Accounts Payable (days).
* ***Total Profit:*** Goal versus strategic plan relative to products, markets, regions, channels, and customers.

As we review the process indicators, we see themes in our approach to measurement goals. The three main themes are time, effort, and performance. In summary, our PI measures and dashboard answer the critical questions:

How hard did we work, how long did it take, and how well did our processes perform?

Similarly, when we review our result indicators, we see themes as well. The three main themes are: revenue in, expenses out, and cash being used to facilitate this overall flow. In summary, our RI measures and dashboard answer the critical question:

What did we earn, what did it cost us to earn this, and how much cash do we have tied up to achieve this result?

To complete our discussion relative to SCA and measures, it is important to recognize several key points. The first is that measures need to be holistic and view the business from an extended value-stream point of view. Second, measures and KPIs are used to guide our work and help us have *the right dialogue about the right business problems at the right time*. Last, we need to recognize that many

> **How hard did we work, how long did it take, and how well did our processes perform?**

KPIs and measures currently in place may in fact contradict extended value-stream thinking, and this should be considered an opportunity to discover hidden profit.

3

Connect the Gears and Mine the Claim

CHAPTER | 12

"… your supply chain is a competitive weapon only if every part of the organization works together on a synchronized basis."

—CHARLIE ARMSTRONG

Implementing SCA is similar to mining for gold. We are the miner who begins as a prospector, a person filled with passion for hard work, skilled in geology and the science of rocks and minerals. We stake a claim after proper research is completed, and we begin to mine. We use known techniques to find a rich vein that will lead to the bonanza of the mother lode. We continue to work the pockets of minerals, being disappointed when we find waste of oreless rock and then encouraged when we strike the free gold that is captured with ease. We extricate the waste to reach the gold behind it and continue to go back for more, moving on to new gold fields and claims when our work is through.

In SCA, our claim is the extended value stream and our research is the connecting of the four core processes of the business. Our skills and knowledge drive supply chain-centric decision making while we mine the Ten Rights across the claim. And our gold is the hidden profit we uncover and extract when we achieve advanced supply-chain performance.

3 SCA Gear 3: Connect the Gears and Mine the Claim:
Extended Value-Stream Improvement Implementation

If we review the first two gears of the SCA machine, we see elements of important preparation required to extract hidden profit from our extended value stream. However, planning and preparation in and of themselves are not a business result. Planning and implementation of SCA operating principles do not have any meaning or value if we don't execute and achieve our goal of advanced supply-chain performance. In addition to actual implementation of SCA, we also need to sustain the efforts and results for the long term. This means we need to embed SCA, advanced supply-chain performance, and extended value-stream thinking into the management system and structure of the organization permanently. We know from experience that the primary reason why business-improvement initiatives are not sustained is because they are on the perimeter of the management system and not considered part of *how we conduct business.*

This embedding of SCA into the management structure of the organization is the purpose of the third SCA Gear.

Figure 27 — *SCA Gear 3: Extended Value-Stream Improvement Implementation*

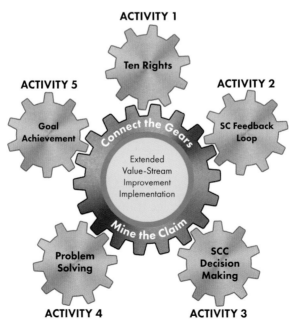

Enabling Activities for SCA Gear 3
Extended Value-Stream Improvement Implementation

* **Gear 3 – Activity 1 |** **Ten Rights:** *Ten Rights-Perspective Design + Implementation*
* **Gear 3 – Activity 2 |** **SC Feedback Loop:** *Supply-Chain Performance Feedback-Loop Implementation*
* **Gear 3 – Activity 3 |** **SCC Decision Making:** *Supply Chain-Centric Decision-Making Execution*
* **Gear 3 – Activity 4 |** **Problem Solving:** *Process-Improvement Capability Evolution*
* **Gear 3 – Activity 5 |** **Goal Achievement:** *Goal Setting + Management-System Alignment*

Gear 3 – Activity 1 | Ten Rights:
Ten Rights-Perspective Design + Implementation

Implementing SCA operating principles and focusing on the Ten Rights is foundational to becoming an extended value-stream thinker. For successful SCA, organizations need to view the business from an "extended value-stream" point of view, where the extended value stream is the *business machine* that is created when we connect the core processes of business strategy, product life-cycle management, sales and marketing, and supply-chain operations. Once accomplished, extended value-stream thinking and visibility of advanced supply-chain performance allows you to see improvement opportunities based on the results of past decisions. With this, we then trace the origins of the decisions back through the core processes in order to make improvements that will lead to better decisions in the future. This is an important essence of SCA as all leaders in an organization need to become Extended Value-Stream Thinkers.

Extended Value-Stream thinking continually asks how current business processes and decisions support the Ten Rights of advanced supply-chain performance. If a process underperforms relative to one of these Ten Rights, it needs to be fixed. If a process doesn't support any of these Ten Rights, it begs the question, *Why are we doing it?* SCA operating principles and management-system structure relentlessly strive towards the Ten Rights to maximize customer value at the lowest possible total cost to the enterprise, all resulting in increased profit. We introduced the concept of the Ten Rights earlier, but let's take some time to dig a little deeper.

As discussed previously, SCA operating principles strive to achieve the Ten Rights from an extended value-stream perspective: 1) the right products, 2) to the right customers, 3) in the right quantities, 4) in the right quality, 5) at the right times, 6) from the right sources (place), 7) at the right prices, 8) at the right total cost, 9) with the right services, 10) all within the right amount of required complexity (effort).

In order to understand the Ten Rights from an extended value-stream point of view, add the words *across the extended value stream* after the right. For example, ask yourself, "How do we ensure we have the right products . . . across the extended value stream?" This elevates the conversation to be business wide as opposed to focusing solely on the last mile of customer delivery.

An important step in understanding SCA, supply chain-centric decision making, and advanced supply-chain performance is for leaders to discuss, document, and align around what the Ten Rights mean for the organization and how the organization will measure performance relative to the Ten Rights.

For example, let's choose the *right product*. Leaders representing all four core processes need to come together and ask themselves:

1. How do we decide what products we want to sell?
2. How do we define and measure what a successful product is?
3. How do we act upon products that are not the right product?
4. What sub-processes exist across the four core processes to ensure we are selling the right product, and how are these processes connected from an extended value-stream point of view to maximize customer value at the lowest possible total cost?

For another example, let's choose the *right quantity*. Leaders representing all four core processes need to ask themselves collaboratively:

1. Relative to this product, how do we decide what quantity to order from our suppliers (lot size), what quantity to manufacture (batch size), what quantity to store (inventory), what quantity to put into a package, and what quantity to replenish when actual customer consumption takes place?

2. How do we gather data and gain visibility as to whether we are disciplined to these ordering quantities and whether the calculations are effective based on actual supply-chain performance?

3. What sub-processes exist across the four core processes to ensure we are inserting the right quantities into the supply chain, and how are these processes connected from an extended value-stream point of view to maximize customer value at the lowest possible total cost?

This technique of asking these questions and embedding the answers in SCA planning processes can be repeated for each of the Ten Rights. We guarantee there will be significant learning and opportunities for business improvement uncovered when this perspective is embedded into the decision-making processes of the organization.

Please beware! As mentioned already, it is absolutely critical at this stage in our discussion that you do not consider the Ten Rights to be the sole responsibility of your supply-chain executives. The Ten Rights represent all four core processes of any business. For example, to ensure we are only developing and producing the *right product* will require input from all four core business processes to ensure we are: developing a product that the customer values, achieving the target cost, creating the proper inventory profiles for the product, positioning and promoting the product in the right location at the right price, and ultimately delivering that particular product when the customer calls. Accomplishing this effectively as measured by *value to the customer at the lowest possible total cost* is a cross-functional collaborative effort. Therefore, the goal is to understand how our four core processes are aligned to achieve the Ten Rights from an extended value-stream and holistic point of view.

> **An important step in understanding SCA, supply chain-centric decision making, and advanced supply-chain performance is for leaders to discuss, document, and align around what the Ten Rights mean for the organization and how the organization will measure performance relative to the Ten Rights.**

Gear 3 – Activity 2 | SC Feedback Loop:
Supply-Chain Performance Feedback-Loop Implementation

A goal of Supply-Chain Advancement is to *leverage advanced supply-chain performance to identify significant improvement opportunities within core business processes.* So, how do we do this? This is accomplished when leaders make supply chain-centric decisions based on a series of known assumptions and then are committed to following up on actual results after implementing our decisions.

For example, through our core-process collaboration, we will determine that we want to sell a particular product to a particular customer in a particular sales channel with a forecasted expectation of sales, revenues, costs, and margins. In addition, we will have collaborated and determined what overall lead times and effort (complexity and supply-chain costs) will be required to sell this product. With this *extended value-stream* based plan set, we will execute together and measure the actual results against the assumptions made in the planning process. That is, once it is operational, we will use actual advanced supply-chain performance to compare plan to actual, question assumptions made, and then use this learning to implement countermeasures and make more effective decisions going forward.

What this means fundamentally is that decision-making processes need to flow in two directions (decision and feedback), and supply-chain operations need to be visible and measurable to the point where the organization gets real facts about *what actually happened as compared to what we thought was going to happen.*

This supply-chain operations feedback loop will need to be installed in the management system of the organization by having a structured review of past decisions made. For example, during an SCA formal review, supply-chain operations will bring the following to the review:

1. Here is a review of a particular product launch, sales promotion, or review of an important high-volume product flow.
2. Here are the assumptions we made relative to the *Ten Rights* and expected business results for this initiative.
3. Here are the agreed-upon extended value-stream KPIs and qualitative information with respect to what actually happened.
4. Here are lessons learned and the key areas we need to prioritize for business-improvement activities across the extended value stream.

5. Here are the recommendations for how we make a similar decision in the future.

This feedback loop is absolutely critical for SCA or any business-improvement initiative to succeed. Executed effectively, this feedback loop will create the necessary *review cycle* within the management system to ensure that all decisions are improved upon based on understanding the gap between our assumptions (what we thought would happen) and true realities of the business environment (what actually happened).

Figure 28 *— Supply-Chain Performance Feedback Loop*

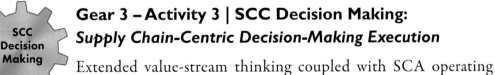

SUPPLY-CHAIN PERFORMANCE FEEDBACK LOOP

Supply-Chain Performance provides feedback for the entire organization relative to decisions made in all parts of the organization.

Gear 3 – Activity 3 | SCC Decision Making:
Supply Chain-Centric Decision-Making Execution

Extended value-stream thinking coupled with SCA operating principles enables Supply Chain-Centric Decision making. Once again (we cannot stress this enough), this is not simply about supply-chain management, and it is not the sole responsibility of supply-chain executives. This is about all four core processes (and sub-processes) of the business understanding and being aligned around the premise that no matter where in the organization a decision is made, the value or waste created by that decision will be manifested in the supply chain. Therefore, *supply chain-centric decision making is simply creating awareness of current and future supply-chain implications in all business decisions.*

Supply chain-centric decision making is a thought process, a procedure or routine we perfect, where we take the probable impact on the supply chain into consideration while making business decisions.

This is a process of *leader-standard work* where we formally and frequently ask ourselves:

* How will this business decision create customer value and support one or more of the Ten Rights?
* How may this business decision create unintended consequences, lead to unplanned (not required) complexity, and drive waste in the supply chain?
* What planned (required) complexity is being created with this business decision, and what knowledge and processes are required to manage this planned complexity?
* How will we objectively measure and validate the assumed value or waste created in the supply chain relative to this business decision?
* How will we create and sustain feedback mechanisms from the supply chain back to the core processes that made the original decisions resulting in the value or waste in the supply chain?
* How will we use this feedback from the supply-chain performance to learn, fix processes, and make better decisions going forward?

The real power of supply chain-centric decision making is that all people inside an organization embrace the fact that you can collectively assess supply-chain performance in order to see and understand, visibly and measurably, the impact of business decisions made from all four core processes of a business. This means that at no point is anybody in the organization simply *down the road and on to new things.* We all stay involved with the actual outcomes of decisions we participated in. This is the essence of true participative management.

This also exemplifies why transparency, visibility, measurement, operating principles, and management systems are so important to successful SCA and the extraction of hidden profit from the supply chain.

Problem Solving

Gear 3 – Activity 4 | Problem Solving: *Process-Improvement Capability Evolution*

Supply-Chain Advancement is considered a business-improvement methodology. This means there is a framework and guiding set of logical steps that can be followed, as we have described throughout the book. Described as a methodology, this also means that you have to adapt SCA thinking to your particular business. Many industries have subtle or significant differences; however, the concepts and principles of SCA can be applied universally when connected to the current strategies of your business. It is very important to us as authors that you recognize we are not advocating a wholesale change in your current strategy. We are advocating that you build upon and augment your current strategy with SCA thinking. And if you complete this work thoughtfully, using voice of customer gathered from the advanced supply-chain performance as your barometer, you will build a sustained culture of extended value-stream based business improvement.

The most important point here is that SCA is a methodology to create a sustained culture of business improvement by using supply-chain performance as a guide to provide improvement opportunities across the entire extended value stream of the business. Yet a challenge that may arise is a situation where the organization does not have the skills or capability to solve problems at the root causes.

A challenge that many organizations face is a lack of formalized business-improvement skills, in particular when it comes to improvements across the entire extended value stream. Consequently, an organization needs to mature in its ability to execute and sustain long-term business improvement for SCA. People inside a business need to learn how to solve problems.

> **We are advocating that you build upon and augment your current strategy with SCA thinking.**

This is a maturing process, where the organization matures in its capability to solve problems effectively. Solving problems effectively means that we have the knowledge to: truly understand the right problem, use relevant data and facts to identify contributing causes and root causes, be creative and forward thinking in our developed solutions, and recognize what the extended value-stream implications will be for the intended solutions.

The following are the stages of problem-solving maturity that we need to progress through in order to achieve Advanced Supply-Chain Performance.

Stage 1 – No Improvement Activity: In this stage, there is no formal business-improvement activity within the organization. The next step is for people within the organization to learn how to make problems visible, and from there they will need to know how to solve functional (local) problems using fundamental tools such as Pareto, 5 Why, Fishbone, and basic project-management tools.

Stage 2 – Functional Improvement: In this stage, improvement activity is focused on waste reduction within a specific function and does not consider any other functions when implementing improvements. An example would be to make improvements within manufacturing while not taking inbound or outbound logistics into consideration relative to their possible impact on the improvements. While functional improvement is valuable and necessary, the challenge is often that the improvements will have unintended consequences in other areas of the business and may at times actually create more waste across the supply chain than that which is being reduced in the functional improvement.

The next step in maturity from functional improvement is to make improvements across the functional value stream, starting with adjacent processes upstream and downstream to the functional process you are focused on.

Stage 3 – Value-Stream Improvement: Within this stage, improvement activities are focused within a core business process, namely business strategy, product life-cycle management, sales and marketing, or supply-chain operations. In this stage, adjacent and connecting sub-processes are considered when implementing improvements. An example would be to make improvements within manufacturing while taking the sub-processes of inbound or outbound logistics into consideration relative to their possible impact on the improvements. The improvement activities would be completed and accomplished by all sub-processes within the core process.

The next step in maturity from value stream improvement is to make improvements across the extended value stream by using SCA implementation steps previously described.

Stage 4 – Extended Value-Stream Improvement: In this stage, improvement activities are focused across all four core processes of the business. The improvement activities are focused on the implementation of agreed-upon operating principles and set goals relative to SCA and Advanced Supply-Chain Performance. This stage of business improvement is the next frontier for significant business results. This is our ultimate goal of SCA.

Figure 29 — *SCA Continuous Improvement Maturity*

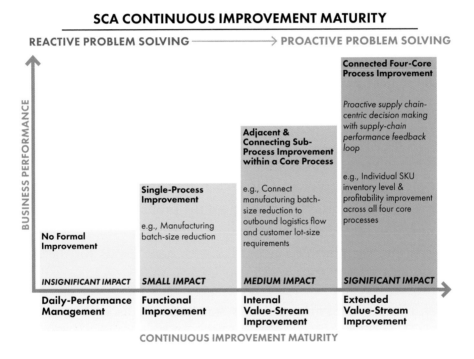

An organization must evolve and mature in its ability for problem solving and continuous improvement across the Extended Value Stream.

It's important to recognize that many organizations are not solely inside one stage of their improvement-capability maturity. That is, they have various levels of maturity depending on functions, divisions, or particular skills of specific leaders. However, for successful implementation of SCA, the organization needs to understand their current maturity level and formalize a plan to develop people and processes to climb the growth curve towards extended value-stream problem-solving capability.

Gear 3 – Activity 5 | Goal Achievement:
Goal Setting + Management-System Alignment

SCA is a fluid business-improvement process. This means we never reach the end, as advanced supply-chain performance provides a continuous feedback loop to identify new business-improvement opportunities. This will be the case as long as we are disciplined to the established management system and review structure. The purpose of the management system is to set goals (targets) and to provide the review processes required to ensure we are reaching these goals. SCA will not be sustained if we do not produce real, measured business results; therefore it is imperative we do the work to achieve planned results and then formally show the business that targeted results were in fact realized.

The management system will create new targets and new challenging goals for the next business period.

This is our last activity, where we come together and say:

1. This was our target for the last business period.
2. This is the work we did, and this is what we achieved.
3. This is what we learned, and these are the problems and opportunities we identified across the extended value stream.
4. This is the recommended action list with new targets for the next business period.

Establishing a powerful management system requires discipline. The discipline to be transparent and honest about the reality of the current state, to set challenging yet realistic improvement targets, to support and implement agreed-upon SCA operating principles, and most importantly, to show up at SCA management-review meetings prepared and with the right attitude to extract hidden profit.

Instilling this level of discipline into the organization will yield unprecedented business results.

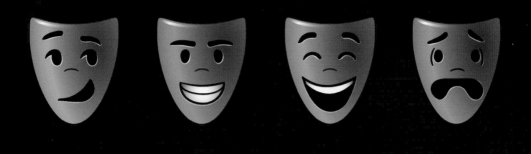

ACT 3

Putting It All Together

Putting It All Together

CHAPTER | 13

"…companies are trying to be more proactive although systemically they haven't developed all of the processes to facilitate a proactive culture."

—ELIJAH RAY

As we approach the end of our explanation of SCA, it's important to pull it all together to show SCA as a methodology, system, or roadmap. We will use this last chapter to walk through the highlights of SCA and outline the path in a way that you can imagine yourself having a conversation with your leadership team. And we hope you actually have this conversation.

SUPPLY-CHAIN ADVANCEMENT | REVIEW AND IMPLEMENTATION ROADMAP

What is Supply-Chain Advancement?

Supply-Chain Advancement (SCA) is a business-improvement methodology that discovers and extracts hidden profit by connecting core business processes to achieve Advanced Supply-Chain Performance.

What is Advanced Supply-Chain Performance?

Advanced Supply-Chain Performance (ASCP) is the business performance we will achieve if we focus our attention on having the right strategy to deliver and sell only the right products while being supported by the right supply-chain operations across the business system wide.

Advanced Supply-Chain Performance is the measured incremental business performance we realize when we connect core business processes and implement supply chain-centric operating principles holistically to achieve the Ten Rights across the extended value stream of the organization, maximizing customer value at the lowest possible total cost to the organization.

Why is SCA important now?

SCA is important right now because it is the way to combat the business disruption that exists today. SCA is the next frontier for business improvement to realize profit that is available to us right now. If we do not connect core processes, complexity and unintended consequences of single-process focused decisions will continue to drive excessive waste into our supply chains, and we will continue to miss out on revenue opportunities.

What do we get if we implement SCA?

We get an organization that is highly collaborative and participative. Processes flow across the extended value stream, and we make supply chain-centric decisions that use advance supply-chain performance as a feed loop to prioritize business-improvement opportunities. We achieve the Ten Rights holistically across the business to generate new revenues at lower operating costs, thereby providing new profit to the business with less overall effort from the organization. In the end, we maximize customer value at the lowest possible total cost to the business.

What is the foundational thinking of SCA?

SCA has several axioms as its foundation.

* **SCA Axiom 1:** All business decisions ultimately are manifested in the supply chain.

* **SCA Axiom 2:** Extended-value stream thinking discovers hidden profit.

* **SCA Axiom 3:** Supply chain-centric decision making will drive extended value-stream thinking and reduce complexity.

* **SCA Axiom 4:** Supply-Chain Advancement enables Advanced Supply-Chain Performance.

* **SCA Axiom 5:** Time is money.

How do I Implement SCA?

The SCA-implementation roadmap has three gears, each with required activities and management methods to be leveraged.

1 SCA Gear 1: Establish Transparency and Demonstrate Full Intent:
Goal Setting + Management-System Alignment

* **Activity 1 | SCA Goals:** *Vision – SCA Macro-Target Setting*
* **Activity 2 | SCA Education:** *SCA Training and Education*
* **Activity 3 | Establishing Management System:** *Management-System Design + Implementation*

2 SCA Gear 2: Remove the Mask and Unite the Cast:
Core-Process Connection + SCA Operating-Principle Implementation

* **Activity 1 | SCA Core-Process Connection:** *Operating-Principle Design + Alignment*
* **Activity 2 | Sub-Processes:** *Sub-Process Identification + Operating Principles*
* **Activity 3 | Methods and Tools:** *Methods and Tools Development + Implementation*
* **Activity 4 | Measurement:** *KPI Development + Target Setting*
* **Activity 5 | Business-Improvement Roadmap:** *Extended Value-Stream Improvement Implementation*

3 SCA Gear 3: Connect the Gears and Mine the Claim:
Extended Value-Stream Improvement Implementation

* **Activity 1 | Ten Rights:** *Ten Rights-Perspective Design + Implementation*
* **Activity 2 | SC Feedback Loop:** *Supply-Chain Performance Feedback-Loop Implementation*
* **Activity 3 | SCC Decision Making:** *Supply Chain-Centric Decision-Making Execution*
* **Activity 4 | Problem Solving:** *Process-Improvement Capability Evolution*
* **Activity 5 | Goal Achievement:** *Goal Setting + Management-System Alignment*

AS PART OF OUR THREE SCA GEARS, THERE ARE ALSO FOUR CRITICAL SCA CORE-PROCESS OPERATING PRINCIPLES:

1. **Business Strategy | SCA as a Differentiating Competency:** SCA and resulting Advanced Supply-Chain Performance are an organizational core competency and strategic market differentiator.

2. **Product Life-Cycle Management | Long-Term Collaborative Product Planning:** Long-term product and sales-channel roadmaps are created collaboratively with simultaneous development of supporting material sourcing, manufacturing, and distribution-planning roadmaps.

3. **Sales and Marketing | Collaborative Demand and Profit Planning:** Highly collaborative customer demand, production, and material planning with a goal of stable and profitable sales growth.

4. **Supply-Chain Operations | Reliable Delivery + Speed and Visible Flow:** Highly reliable delivery and capable speed with end-to-end supply-chain visibility focuses on implementing and controlling leveled flow and velocity across an extremely stable and reliable logistics network.

There are also Key Performance Indicators, all with the goal of achieving:

The Ten Rights: 1) the right products, 2) to the right customers, 3) in the right quantities, 4) in the right quality, 5) at the right times, 6) from the right sources, 7) at the right prices, 8) at the right total cost, 9) with the right services, 10) all within the right amount of required complexity (effort) across the extended value stream.

Achieving the Ten Rights will ultimately yield the business result of:

Extracting hidden profit by maximizing customer value at the lowest possible total cost to the business.

SCA Success

CONCLUSION

"If you know, but you don't do, then you don't really know."

—ARISTOTLE

First and foremost, thank you for your time and interest in Supply-Chain Advancement. We hope with all sincerity that you see value in embracing SCA as a methodology to extract hidden profit that is currently available to you. All that is left is to act, to embrace SCA, and to understand how it will embed within your current operations.

We need to *Establish Transparency and Demonstrate Full Intent* in order to see the business for what it truly is and engage our entire work force in this extremely important work.

We need to *Remove the Mask and Unite the Cast* to connect core processes and allow our talented leaders, managers, and team members to utilize their full potential across the entire business as a total system.

We need to *Connect the Gears and Mine the Claim,* discover and extract all profit that is available to us and that has been rightfully earned by focusing on maximizing value to our customers at the lowest possible total cost.

If we now retrace our steps back to the introduction, as authors we made several promises and we asked for a few favors.

We asked that you appreciate that this is not a book about supply-chain management, but rather is a book about business management, focusing on overall business performance. As well, we asked that you share the ideas in this book with all executives inside your organization in order to begin the journey of cross-functional, business-wide extended value-stream thinking. Last, we asked you not to reject SCA as being *too hard* to implement. As authors, we still remain steadfast that this work may very well determine which organizations survive and thrive in the coming decades.

As for promises made, we first promised not to inundate you with concepts and theories that are not practical to implement. We hope that we were able to accomplish this goal by articulating SCA in a common-sense fashion, showing SCA as a methodology with clear and actionable steps that can be implemented in any organization or industry.

Second, we promised that SCA can build upon your current strategies and leverage any work you have completed to develop a culture of business improvement. Again, we hope we have accomplished this goal by showing that SCA does not require an abrupt shift in strategy. Instead we simply advocate a participative and collaborative approach to decision making where we take implications for the supply chain into consideration as we complete work across the extended value stream.

Last, we promised that real, measurable, and significant business results will derive from implementing SCA. We admitted that it will not always be easy, but focusing on Supply-Chain Advancement will take you to the next level of business performance required in today's world of constant disruption.

We now need your help to fulfill this promise.

We need you to lead SCA within your organization, for no other reason than it's simply the right thing to do to discover hidden profit.

ACT 4

Hearing the Voices of Cast Members

The following interviews were completed by David Drickhamer.

We would like to thank David, along with Sue Armstrong,
Michael Edmunds, Charlie Armstrong, Rick Sather,
Elijah Ray, Rick Blasgen and Heather Sheehan.

Your insight, experience and wisdom will allow organizations
to solve the big business problems of the next decade.

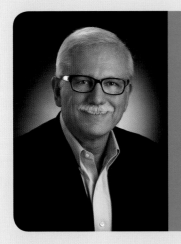

CHARLES ARMSTRONG is a Founding Partner of Orion Advisors Group. He has over 30 years of experience as a senior executive in distribution and manufacturing network design, supply-chain optimization, international logistics, facility planning and design, leadership development, organizational design and performance optimization. Previously he held senior leadership P&L positions in the retail, hospitality, manufacturing, and consulting industries.

LEVERAGE YOUR SUPPLY CHAIN AS A COMPETITIVE WEAPON

A conversation with Charles Armstrong, Partner, Orion Advisors Group.

Q: CAN YOU TALK ABOUT WHAT SUPPLY CHAINS LOOK LIKE TODAY AND HOW THEY NEED TO PERFORM?

Early in my career we talked about having the right product at the right price and being able to supply from anywhere and ship to anywhere at any time. Those were conceptual conversations at that time, but in the past decade we've rapidly moved to implement that vision.

Now we can manage inventories around the world and have visibility of everything that's on order and in production. Consumer expectations today are exceeding many organizations' capabilities because of the speed at which these changes have occurred.

The need for integration between departments is significantly higher because of the speed and the rate at which capabilities can change. It also requires a level of planning that, quite frankly, didn't exist in the past.

Q: WHAT ARE SOME OF THE BARRIERS TO MORE EFFECTIVE SUPPLY-CHAIN PLANNING AND INTEGRATION?

The traditional supply chain optimized the individual components: procurement, transportation, inventory, planning, distribution, outbound or delivery operations. Inventory moved through the supply chain as a series of independent events. At each point in that process, there was wasted time, wasted cost, wasted handling, and wasted space. That's the opposite of a lean supply chain that operates with minimal lead times and minimal variances on a consistent basis.

One side effect that we're seeing are DCs and supply chains that are at or above capacity because of the rate at which organizations are adding new SKUs. There is a disconnect in accountability for the capacity or the expense associated with the infrastructure for supporting all those SKUs: the new, the old, the slow turn, and the dead. As a result, you end up with a supply chain that is challenged with capacity and velocity issues and an inability to effectively fulfill customer orders because of a lack of planning and poor end-to-end integration.

Q: CAN YOU DESCRIBE SOME OF THE SOLUTIONS TO THESE SUPPLY-CHAIN CHALLENGES?

In order to carry as many SKUs as possible and maximize customer service, you have to carry as little inventory as possible of any given SKU. That requires sophisticated forecasting and planning that integrates lead times throughout the supply chain. A synchronized planning process determines what levels are required to meet the desired service levels. Manufacturers' lead times, transportation times, process times through distribution, fulfillment, and delivery are all taken into consideration.

By reducing the cycle time, we reduce the peaks and valleys, eliminate excess and under inventory, and maximize service levels. That maximizes inventory turnover at the minimum total cost.

Today, most distribution centers are, or should be, operating with a paperless receiving process. They pre-receive product prior to its actual arrival and are performing some form of dynamic reallocation of inventory prior to receipt. That didn't occur in the past because there wasn't a demand for it, and the information support wasn't there to support flow through processing.

Q: HOW CAN COMPANIES LEVERAGE THEIR SUPPLY CHAINS FOR A COMPETITIVE ADVANTAGE?

Using your supply chain as a competitive weapon only occurs when every part of the organization works together on a synchronized basis. That means creating an understanding throughout the organization on how the various components of a supply chain are integrated with each other and how they need to share information in order to maximize the benefit. That never occurs unless leadership at the highest level endorses an end-to-end way of doing business.

Q: SO IT ALL COMES DOWN TO LEADERSHIP?

In my last corporate role, the greatest contributing factor to the success of our supply chain transformation was an end-to-end commitment from senior management on down. Everyone was committed to creating a supply chain that improved lead times, reduced in-transit times, and operated in a more cost-effective manner. If it weren't for those common goals, we would not have been successful.

SUE ARMSTRONG is Chief Operations Officer of Nature's Sunshine Products. She is responsible for worldwide sourcing, manufacturing, distribution, and information technology. Previously she worked in senior operational leadership roles for Metagenics, Carl Zeiss Vision, and Great Lakes Chemical Corp.

SUPPLY-CHAIN PERFORMANCE MEASUREMENT AND VISIBILITY ARE ESSENTIAL FOR CROSS-FUNCTIONAL ALIGNMENT.

A conversation with Sue Armstrong, Chief Operations Officer of Nature's Sunshine Products.

Q: BASED ON YOUR OBSERVATIONS AND EXPERIENCE, WHAT ARE SOME OF THE WAYS THAT MARKET COMPLEXITY IS AFFECTING SUPPLY-CHAIN PERFORMANCE?

For most organizations, more SKUs means smaller manufacturing lots and increased changeovers. That's a challenge from a manufacturing, planning, and inventory point of view, which drives the need for agility.

One of the issues increasing demand complexity in our industry is the risk of obsolescence, because most products have a two-year shelf life. We're also seeing increasing complexity globally from regulations.

Q: WHAT ARE SOME OF THE CHALLENGES TO MANAGING SUCH COMPLEXITY?

Complexity increases the importance for manufacturers to be closely aligned with key strategic suppliers and be more vertically integrated to be assured of the ingredient and the raw material supply. Depending on the maturity of the organization and how good their S&OP process is, a poor forecast can really wreak havoc on the supply chain in terms of effectiveness and cost management.

Another major issue is having late decisions during new product launches. Decisions late in the product lifecycle and stage-gate process negate a lot of the work that's already done. Packaging decisions, label design, or branding changes late in the timeline can really impact the cost effectiveness of the launch.

Q: WHAT ARE SOME OF THE WAYS TO MANAGE THAT COMPLEXITY AND TAKE A MORE PROACTIVE APPROACH TO SUPPLY-CHAIN MANAGEMENT?

Cross-functional alignment is absolutely critical in any company. Sales, marketing, operations, and R&D need to be fully aligned. Everyone in the business must be clear on what the priorities are.

S&OP processes are the backbone. A really good S&OP process connects the key functions together within any organization. It establishes a monthly cadence of activity whereby the tactical plans are realigned with the business unit in the short- and long-term.

For new-product activity and anything that's changing within a company, executive attendance is important. You have to make sure that you're very, very focused from the top on the key priorities for the business and that resources are aligned.

It's a challenge to align the sales and supply-chain teams. If decisions increase consumer-demand complexity, you have to make sure that it doesn't have a negative impact on the overall margin of the business.

Q: AS A SENIOR OPERATIONS LEADER, HOW DO YOU ENCOURAGE THAT UNDERSTANDING AND SUPPLY-CHAIN DECISION MAKING AMONG MANAGERS AND EMPLOYEES AT ALL LEVELS?

When I came here there was a lack of visible, aligned, and coordinated metrics, no balanced scorecards, nothing on the walls. Now, it's a very visual organization. We have customer-facing metrics, financial metrics, internal business-process metrics, and learning and growth metrics. Every morning we have a cross-functional huddle when we talk about where we are, the issues, and what we need to focus on.

It's important that my colleagues in marketing, sales, R&D, etc., can see how the supply chain is performing and, step-by-step, make sure that we're all working more in sync to the targets.

The silo mentality kills supply-chain efficiency. This is not a competition between departments. It makes work a fun place to be when everyone comes together.

Q: IN THIS BOOK WE'VE DESCRIBED HOW A SUPPLY CHAIN-CENTRIC OPERATING APPROACH INCLUDES: OPTIMIZING VISIBILITY, VALUE-STREAM THINKING, FOCUSING ON LEAD-TIME REDUCTIONS, QUALITY AT THE SOURCE, AND OTHER CORE PRINCIPLES. WHAT WOULD YOU EMPHASIZE?

You also have to create the appropriate environment where people develop and progress. That means creating an atmosphere where people want to contribute and know that they're valued. Our success has had everything to do with culture, continuous improvement, and being a coaching organization. While those other key principles are absolutely needed, I don't think organizations are successful in supply chain unless they've got the culture piece as well.

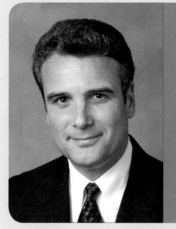

RICK D. BLASGEN is President and Chief Executive Officer of the Council of Supply Chain Management Professionals (CSCMP). He is responsible for the overall business operations and strategic plan of the organization. Previously he was Senior Vice President Integrated Logistics at ConAgra Foods, Vice President Supply Chain at Kraft, and Vice President Supply Chain at Nabisco.

SUPPLY-CHAIN ALIGNMENT STARTS WITH ALIGNING SENIOR LEADERSHIP OBJECTIVES AND INCENTIVES

A conversation with Rick Blasgen, President and CEO, CSCMP

Q: HOW DOES IMPROVING SUPPLY-CHAIN PERFORMANCE HAVE A DIRECT IMPACT ON BUSINESS PERFORMANCE?

If you finance less inventory in your supply chain, that's less interest expense that you have to spend. So that's a P&L impact. I used to run models where we turned inventory faster and created cash flow that could be redeployed to other parts of the company. To do that, you need to forecast better. You need to share promotional information better so you can anticipate how to position inventory better. If you can do things with your supply chain that your competition is either unwilling to do or incapable of doing, your business should go up.

Q: WHAT ARE SOME OF THE CHALLENGES TO INSTILLING A SUPPLY-CHAIN MINDSET THROUGHOUT A BUSINESS?

If you go to a senior leader who is primarily a brand person brought up on the marketing side and talk about a seamless and fluid supply chain or satisfying the needs of customers at the lowest total delivered cost they're not going to know what you're talking about.

You may think your CEO knows how products flow from the point of manufacturer to a customer's shelf, but they may not. Supply-chain leaders have to be internal salespeople. They have to talk intelligently in a language everyone can understand. For example, "If we implement this better warehousing network, our earnings per share is going to go up."

Q: WHAT ARE SOME OF THE BARRIERS THAT STAND IN THE WAY OF MANAGERS MAKING DECISIONS THAT TAKE THE SUPPLY-CHAIN IMPLICATIONS INTO CONSIDERATION?

I don't think we've done enough around aligning the goals and objectives of top executives to ensure supply-chain excellence is easily achieved. I once looked at the goals and bonuses of every functional head of our company: manufacturing, procurement, marketing, sales, and logistics. They were clearly in conflict.

For example, the bonus objectives of a procurement professional in any company are unlikely to include inventory turns or customer service or on-time delivery. They will focus on economic order quantity, reduction of procurement costs, first-time yield, and other back-of-the-house metrics. Doing these well might improve the supply chain, but they're not necessarily in alignment with the goals and objectives of someone who is customer facing.

I'll never forget, in our soup business we suddenly started seeing a lot of damage in our distribution centers, and our customer returns of these cans of soup were increasing. It turned out that they had reduced the thickness of the can, claiming who knows how many millions of dollars in savings, but that was superseded by all of the damaged product.

Q: HOW CAN SOME OF THESE ALIGNMENT CHALLENGES BE OVERCOME?

One way is to include supply-chain people in the stage-gate process for new product development. They're in there making sure the R&D people don't create some unintended consequences.

Sales and operations planning has been around for a long time. It's difficult to implement, but when it is implemented, it does drive better behavior.

Senior-level executives, who may not want to get into the weeds, have to understand that their presence and involvement in supply-chain activities has a significant impact on performance.

MICHAEL EDMUNDS is Vice President of Manufacturing and Global Supply Chain (MGSC) of Bose. His functional areas of responsibility include manufacturing, global supply planning and distribution, global supply management, strategic alliance, and global quality. He has over 25 years of global experience in a wide range of disciplines including procurement, supply chain, manufacturing engineering, quality, operations management, and lean enterprise. Previously he held leadership positions in the nuclear energy, commercial lighting, automotive, and heavy-duty industrial business sectors.

SUPPLY-CHAIN ADVANCEMENT DRIVES HORIZONTAL ALIGNMENT AND CUSTOMER FOCUS

A conversation with Michael Edmunds, Vice President of Manufacturing and Global Supply Chain, Bose Corp.

Q: WHY DOES SUPPLY-CHAIN ADVANCEMENT AND SUPPLY-CHAIN IMPROVEMENT MATTER NOW?

Look at what it takes to get to market today with e-commerce. Almost nothing. That's why we have to accelerate new ideas and new products horizontally across our business. We have to have business models that allow us to operate quickly.

It comes down to value creation for the customer. If we truly look at it through the lens of our customers, they don't care what goes on inside the business. They want the value, and that's why we're in business.

Q: WE'VE WRITTEN ABOUT RISING SUPPLY-CHAIN COMPLEXITY. WHAT'S DRIVING THE TREND FROM YOUR PERSPECTIVE?

Buying behaviors and channel disparity—the so-called omni-channel—are driving a lot of chaos across the supply chain. That dynamic isn't going away. Look at where we're headed – making deliveries within hours in certain markets, which allows consumers to further postpone buying.

When you look at it on a global scale, in Asia for example, they want the same thing. So supply-chain complexity is compounding.

Q: HOW DO YOU CLARIFY THAT CHALLENGE FROM A SUPPLY-CHAIN DESIGN AND MANAGEMENT PERSPECTIVE?

We work backwards from the customer. Looking at the entire value chain, we break it into sales and marketing on the front end, which leads to the customer, the supply chain, and then product development. Those three elements make up the value chain. It's a three-dimensional model.

Q: CONNECTING THOSE FUNCTIONAL ELEMENTS OF A VALUE CHAIN CAN BE HARD. HOW DO YOU GET PEOPLE TO WORK TOGETHER TO OPTIMIZE THE WHOLE IN TERMS OF SUPPLY-CHAIN DECISION MAKING?

We leverage maturity models to understand the business processes across the value chain and to determine how we transition from being reactive to more proactive. We want to connect vertical functional excellence to the horizontal value chain. These maturity models allow us to see where we're at.

We're fortunate that, as a diversified company, we're at different levels within each of our businesses. That's allowed us to leverage best practices across our businesses to drive the value.

Q: CAN YOU TALK ABOUT SOME OF THE PRACTICES THAT HELP MAKE YOUR VALUE CHAINS MORE PROACTIVE?

We leverage business alliance councils that look at the verticals and the horizontals together. They help develop a strategy and action plans that counter the gaps that create friction and make it more difficult for us to accelerate value across the horizontal dimension. There's a lot of competing and conflicting work that goes on, but that forum provides the structure and charters to advance value-chain maturity and, ultimately, deliver better performance.

Q: WITHIN THIS CONTEXT, WHAT DOES SUPPLY-CHAIN ADVANCEMENT LOOK LIKE IN TERMS OF LEADERSHIP?

Think about the scope of responsibilities just within supply chain where you may have supply-and-demand planning, procurement, distribution, and manufacturing. You've got to cross-pollinate and cross-train leadership in all of those subsets of the supply chain. And then, as you step up, you've got to look across all of the functions to drive end-to-end horizontal value.

Ultimately, when you look at the evolution of the value chain, future business leaders have to understand all three dimensions in order to be successful. Compared to those that are only one- or two-dimensional, leaders that understand all three verticals can do incredible things to help scale and prioritize the work across the value chain.

ELIJAH RAY is Executive Vice President, Customer Solutions of Sunland Logistics. He specializes in operations excellence, quality, customer-relationship development, marketing, and sales. Previously a Former CSCMP President, he has over 25 dedicated years in the field of Logistics and Supply-Chain Management with a focus on operations excellence, quality, customer-relationship development, marketing, and sales.

PLENTY OF OPPORTUNITIES REMAIN FOR SUPPLY-CHAIN ADVANCEMENTS THAT IMPROVE CUSTOMER SERVICE AND REDUCE COSTS

A conversation with Elijah Ray, Executive Vice President, Sunland Logistics.

Q: WHAT ARE SOME OF THE MAJOR SUPPLY-CHAIN TRENDS FROM YOUR PERSPECTIVE AS A SENIOR LEADER OF A THIRD-PARTY LOGISTICS PROVIDER?

Our profession is undergoing a major shift. We buy more online, and we want it tomorrow; we want our orders yesterday. That creates complexity, smaller orders, and smaller shipment quantities. Smaller shipments require more labor in the warehouse. They require more precision to get product where it needs to be, when it needs to be there, in good condition.

Q: HOW IS SUPPLY-CHAIN MANAGEMENT CHANGING IN RESPONSE TO THESE MARKET CHANGES?

CEOs now realize the importance of the supply chain. There's a lot more strategic decision making and strategic planning, and there is a lot less waste. Senior supply-chain people are driving key performance indicators – inventory and the carrying costs associated with it – that really impact financial performance.

Some companies have become really good at supply-chain management. We still have companies that are just not as focused on quality and continuous improvement. But from an overall supply-chain perspective, we are maturing and we are growing. Companies are trying to be more proactive although systemically they haven't developed all of the processes to facilitate a proactive culture.

Q: AS A 3PL, YOU HAVE AN INTERESTING VIEW OF SOME OF THE SUPPLY-CHAIN DISCONNECTS AND OPPORTUNITIES BETWEEN ORGANIZATIONS. CAN YOU OFFER ANY EXAMPLES?

Procurement often has a lot of power in organizations, compared to the operations team, for example, who tend to be closer to customers and know the business better. Procurement may select a provider based on a price that appears lower. But then the company doesn't get the complete services that they need because procurement doesn't completely understand logistics, supply chain, warehousing, and value-added services. This happens a lot and it creates real issues.

We have products sitting in our warehouse because we're waiting on the corrugate to re-package it. The company uses a corrugate partner overseas, and it takes us forever to get it over here. All the while there's a corrugate manufacturer within five minutes of our facility that could make and supply the corrugate, which would dramatically reduce their inventory and keep the product flowing.

Q: HOW DO YOU COMMUNICATE AND RECTIFY ISSUES LIKE THAT, WHICH WOULD OPTIMIZE BOTH SUPPLY-CHAIN PERFORMANCE AND COST?

We have business reviews with our key contacts and our shippers when we share information about things like that which don't make sense at the floor level. Most of the companies that we deal with now have fairly sophisticated continuous improvement efforts.

Q: ANY OTHER SOLUTIONS FOR MANAGING COMPLEXITY AND TAKING A MORE PROACTIVE APPROACH TO SUPPLY-CHAIN MANAGEMENT AND IMPROVEMENT?

Some companies are much slower than others. They're just not as focused on inventory carrying costs as they are other areas of the supply chain.

The more that we collaborate within the supply chain and between the various other functions, the more effective we're going to be.

If the CEO is focused on supply-chain improvement, the company will be focused on it. Even if the CEO is not, but he or she has a champion at the senior level who is focused on supply-chain issues, then it becomes a priority.

Q: WHY SHOULD ANY CEO BE FOCUSED ON SUPPLY CHAIN AND LOGISTICS PERFORMANCE?

The last time I benchmarked it, logistics was somewhere between 6% and 8% of sales. That's fairly significant, which makes it a priority.

Logistics presents a tremendous opportunity to provide better customer service. On-time delivery is huge. The most important KPI to a customer is getting the product when they want to get it.

Some companies are now looking at their inventory, at their supply chain, where products are coming in, and their final destinations. That's a huge opportunity to take costs out.

RICK SATHER is Vice President, Supply Chain and Operations, at Jack Link's Protein Snacks. He is responsible for all customer-facing supply chain (customer service, logistics/transportation, and distribution), manufacturing, operations planning (demand and supply), and procurement. Previously he held positons of VP, progressive functional and leadership roles in supply chain and logistics operations during his 29-year tenure at Kimberly Clark. He is a recipient of the Shingo Prize Research and Professional Publication Award for his co-authored book *Lean RFS (Repetitive Flexible Supply): Putting the Pieces Together.*

THE SUPPLY CHAIN PROVIDES THE DISCIPLINE AND GUIDANCE FOR MARKET SUCCESS

A conversation with Rick Sather, Vice President, Supply Chain and Operations of Jack Link's Protein Snacks.

Q: HOW CAN FUNCTIONAL AND BUSINESS UNIT MANAGERS INCORPORATE SUPPLY-CHAIN THINKING INTO THEIR DECISION-MAKING PROCESSES IN WAYS THAT BENEFIT THE ENTIRE ENTERPRISE?

The role of supply-chain and operations leaders is not just to be responsive and manage the basic metrics we're accountable for. We have to bridge the internal cross-functional gaps with Sales, Marketing, R&D, Finance, IT, and external partners to deliver service, quality, and cost results for the company.

In a high-growth company, supply chain enables growth. In my current role I sit with our leaders of sales, marketing, and other functional areas. Bringing these functional groups together to work effectively starts with having compelling business reasons for change.

Q: MANY COMPANIES ARE STRUGGLING TO MANAGE THE INCREASED SUPPLY-CHAIN COMPLEXITY DRIVEN BY CHANGING CUSTOMER EXPECTATIONS. WHAT IMPACT IS THIS COMPLEXITY HAVING ON SUPPLY-CHAIN STRATEGY AND EXECUTION FROM YOUR PERSPECTIVE?

Companies have to become more nimble and create customization capabilities that differentiate your products. That makes complexity a growth enabler, not just something to complain about.

Q: HOW CAN SUPPLY-CHAIN LEADERS TAKE A PROACTIVE APPROACH AND DRIVE SUPPLY-CHAIN AND BUSINESS IMPROVEMENT?

You have to look at the current state and future state, understand where the performance gaps are, and then realize which ones are going to be hard and easy to tackle.

Fundamentally, the supply-chain operational leadership role is being a disciplinarian who builds credibility by performing well and spotlighting the things that you can do to be a more successful company. If your supply-chain performance is weak, then these cross-functional opportunities are hard to get at.

Q: WHAT ARE SOME OF THE CHALLENGES AND OPPORTUNITIES FOR INSTILLING SUPPLY CHAIN-CENTRIC OPERATING PRINCIPLES INTO A COMPANY'S MANAGEMENT AND LEADERSHIP SYSTEMS?

I want to build our capability to improve at a faster rate than my competition. No matter where I'm at, if my rate of improvement is faster than who I'm competing with, then I know I'm going to win.

Building that capability comes down to creating a problem-solving culture and engaging people in their work in a way where they can make a difference. It's simple to say but very hard to do.

I've seen some examples of good operations based purely on the skills of a super leader who has the breadth and depth to keep things afloat and drive good performance. But the minute that leader is gone, it falls apart if there's not a built-in system. Your people have to get better at exposing and solving problems that don't boil up into bigger problems, which takes more skill and expertise from higher-ups to address.

Q: WHAT ARE SOME OF THE FUNCTIONAL BARRIERS TO ADOPTING A BROADER SUPPLY-CHAIN MINDSET?

I wouldn't single out a particular function as much as individuals in those functions. Fundamentally, it comes down to how they are measured and their experience.

If I'm in sales and measured purely on top line with no other measures, it will be different from someone who's measured based on margin or market share. So measurement matters, and people's backgrounds matter.

HEATHER SHEEHAN is retired Vice President, Indirect Sourcing and Logistics, Danaher Corporation. As Danaher's co-Chief Procurement Officer, she had worldwide responsibility for non-production and logistics sourcing, strategy, and implementation across the corporation's 40-plus operating companies. Previously Heather held various leadership positions in procurement, logistics, and marketing with Honeywell, Union Pacific Corporation, and NCR Corporation.

HOW THE SUPPLY CHAIN IMPACTS BOTH THE COST AND REVENUE SIDE OF THE PROFIT EQUATION

A conversation with Heather Sheehan,
former co-Chief Procurement Officer, Danaher Corp.

Q: BUSINESS DECISIONS THAT TAKE THE SUPPLY-CHAIN IMPLICATIONS INTO ACCOUNT CAN HAVE A DIRECT IMPACT ON SUPPLY-CHAIN PERFORMANCE AND BUSINESS PERFORMANCE. WHAT PREVENTS MORE MANAGERS FROM MAKING SUPPLY CHAIN-CENTRIC DECISIONS?

There's often a misalignment of objectives and measures of success between different functional areas. Here's a simple example. Marketing and sales departments are focused on the top line. They have their objectives around growing market share and growing revenue. On the other side, the supply-chain function is expected to drive down cost and provide procurement savings. They don't speak the same language, which creates goal misalignment.

Q: HOW CAN COMPANIES MANAGE SUCH CONFLICTS AND OPTIMIZE DECISIONS AT AN ENTERPRISE-WIDE LEVEL?

Different functional areas have to make decisions that take into account the impact on other functional areas. They have to quickly understand "cost to serve" and the impact on customers of changes in the supply chain, as well as what competitors are doing.

With regard to costs, there has to be both pre-decision information and post-audits of those decisions. For example, the decision might be to serve a customer with 80% of shipments by ground and 20% by air. You have to go back and look at how it actually turns out, which might be the exact opposite.

Including supply-chain representation on new-product introduction and launch teams can also be effective. That's atypical, but it can make a big difference. Many products can be very difficult to ship because of their design. Designing them from the beginning so they are configured for shipping purposes is often better for handling, damage prevention, and overall logistics cost.

Q: HOW DOES IMPROVING SUPPLY-CHAIN PERFORMANCE IMPROVE BUSINESS PERFORMANCE?

Ultimately it's about the bottom line: profitability. There are two sides to that: the revenue side and the cost side. The supply chain plays in both.

It's easy to understand the impact of supply-chain performance on the cost side. But one of the challenges for any company is to make supply chain a competitive advantage that drives the top line as well. A customer's buying decision starts with the tangible product, its features and benefits, its performance and quality. But availability, delivery, and service have significant influence on buyers' decisions. Those factors can make buyers less price sensitive and help a business grow revenue and market share.

Q: WHAT CAN SENIOR MANAGEMENT DO TO INCREASE CONSIDERATION OF THE SUPPLY-CHAIN IMPLICATIONS AND TRADEOFFS DURING DECISION MAKING?

Alignment is absolutely critical. If the top level goals and strategies are not well communicated by senior leaders, that makes tradeoff decisions much more difficult and creates misalignment and conflict within the organization. There are different supply-chain strategies. There are different go-to-market strategies. There are different customer-service strategies. They all involve tradeoffs. If senior leaders have clearly communicated the company's strategic priorities throughout the organization, then managers and front-line employees can execute good, deliberate decisions around those tradeoffs.

The other piece is speed. I've worked in a handful of Fortune 500 companies over my career. The ones that have had the least amount of bureaucracy, that have empowered people with the information to make decisions, are the ones that make decisions faster. That's better for the customer and better for the company.

PETER J MARKS

Peter J. Marks, CEO of Executive Consultant which he founded in 2013, advises business leaders on leadership and strategy development. He is also an Independent Director at Broadcom Limited and serves on the boards of several private companies.

Previously Peter served in various senior management roles with Robert Bosch GmbH, which he originally joined in 1977 and where he remained until December 2011. Most recently, from 2006 until his departure in December 2011, Peter served as Chairman, President, and Chief Executive Officer of Robert Bosch LLC where he managed all of its business sectors in the Americas. He was a member of the Board of Management of Robert Bosch GmbH with responsibility for worldwide coordination for manufacturing and capital investment.

Peter can be reached at peter12912@hotmail.com

ROBERT O. MARTICHENKO

Robert O. Martichenko is Founder and CEO of LeanCor Supply Chain Group, a trusted supply-chain partner whose mission is *To Advance the World's Supply Chains*. Robert's entire career has been committed to third-party logistics, and he has spent over 20 years learning and implementing lean and operational excellence with a focus on end-to-end supply-chain management.

In addition to leading LeanCor, Robert is a senior instructor for the Lean Enterprise Institute and the Georgia Tech Supply Chain and Logistics Institute, a frequent speaker for professional industry groups, and a board member for a private company.

As recognition for his contribution to supply-chain management, Robert received the 2015 Distinguished Service Award from the Council of Supply Chain Management Professionals (CSCMP).

Robert has written several lean and supply-chain books and articles – most notably *Everything I Know About Lean I Learned in First Grade* and two Shingo Research Award winning books, *People*: *A leader's day-to-day guide to building, managing and sustaining lean organizations* and *Building a Lean Fulfillment Stream* (Lean Enterprise Institute).

Robert can be reached at rmartichenko@leancor.com